THE LITTLE
BOOK OF THE

PARANORMAL

RUPERT
MATTHEWS

First published 2010

The History Press
The Mill, Brimscombe Port
Stroud, Gloucestershire, GL5 2QG
www.thehistorypress.co.uk

British Library Cataloguing in Publication Data.
A catalogue record for this book is available from the British Library.

ISBN 978 0 7524 5165 7
Typesetting and origination by The History Press
Printed in Great Britain

CONTENTS

INTRODUCTION

Scientists would have us believe that the world is all sorted out and explained. They have split the atom, landed men on the Moon and explained the inner workings of the human body. They give the impression that there is nothing that cannot be adequately explained by the laws of physics. When something is reported that appears to go beyond the normal, to be 'paranormal', the average scientist will ignore it.

The train of thought goes that because there is no scientific explanation for ghosts or poltergeists or UFOs it must logically follow that such things do not exist; because nobody has ever shot dead a Yeti and brought its body back for scientific study it must mean that the creature itself does not exist; and because those who claim to have magnetic bodies lose that ability within a few days it must mean that they never had such power. It is not a very big leap of logic to take to then denounce all those who report such phenomena as being fools, charlatans or worse.

It is, of course, a safe and cosy world view to adopt. By believing that everything has been explained, those scientists avoid the need to accept that the universe is a rather stranger place than they suppose.

And yet, from time to time, things happen that shake that world view. For centuries peasants, labourers and others reported that they sometimes found rocks that seemed to have fallen from the sky. Some went so far as to say that the rock in question had come crashing through the roofs of their houses at enormous speed. They were all ignored. How could a wind, however strong, pick up a rock weighing over 30 pounds and then dump it on some unsuspecting peasant's house? The whole idea was ridiculous and was written off as nonsense, while those who reported falling rocks were viewed as being liars or idiots to be so easily duped by some practical joke. And then a great rock came crashing through the roof of the house of a German scientist named Ernst Florens Chladni. The subject had to be taken seriously, and fairly soon the scientists had worked out that the falling rocks had come from outer space. They were dubbed 'meteorites'. Scientists went on to write learned treatises on meteorites, their origins and their behaviour. The scientists enjoyed the plaudits of their fellows, but of course the poor peasants who had been labelled liars and fools never received any sort of apology.

That is not to say that all reports of the paranormal are true, nor that science is always wrong. It does show, however, that even the most poorly educated person is capable of faithfully reporting a strange event. And such reports continue to be made. Thousands of people claim to have seen a UFO, tens of thousands have experienced a poltergeist visitation and millions claim to have seen a ghost. One does not have to subscribe to the idea that UFOs are spaceships from some fantastically futuristic alien civilisation to accept that the reports made by different people are both consistent and credible.

The 'normal' world out there is not really so normal at all. There are a great many paranormal features that need to be explained. This book contains just a few.

1

UFOS & ALIENS

For many years people have been seeing strange objects flying through the sky. Known today as UFOs (Unidentified Flying Objects), these phenomena have gone by various names in the past: flying saucers, flying discs, secret airships, foo fighters, ghost rockets and other names have all been used. As yet there has been no widely accepted explanation for what these objects might be. That has not stopped people from putting ideas forward.

In the 1890s flying objects that flew faster and higher than any balloons or airships known to mankind were sighted over the USA and elsewhere. The newspapers at the time suggested that there was a very rich inventor living somewhere in the USA who had invented a new type of airship. They thought the inventor might be testing his airship in secret and predicted that he would one day reveal it to the world, but he never did.

In 1944 an RAF air crew operating over Europe at night reported seeing mysterious glowing balls that followed their aircraft, swooping and diving around the night sky at amazing speeds. At first it was thought the objects were some kind of German secret weapon. They were dubbed 'foo fighters' by the air crew, who tried to shoot them down or manoeuvre away from them – but always without success. After the war it was discovered that the Germans had also encountered the foo fighters, but had thought they were British secret weapons.

In 1946 a series of unexplained objects flew through the skies over Sweden, Norway and Finland. Those who saw the objects thought that they might be rockets being test fired from Soviet Russia. When it was realised that no trace of the rockets crashing to the ground was ever found, the objects were dubbed ghost rockets because they vanished as soon as they were sighted.

Later, on 24 June 1947, an American businessman named Kenneth Arnold was flying home from a business meeting in Washington State. As he passed close to Mount Rainier, Arnold sighted a group of unusual aircraft. The craft were about the size of normal aircraft, but instead of having a fuselage and wings they were shaped like crescents. The mysterious craft were flying at speeds far in excess of anything a man-made aircraft could achieve and following an odd undulating motion. Arnold worried that the aircraft might be top secret Soviet bombers and reported the sighting to the FBI when he landed. He also spoke to local newspapers, saying that the craft flew 'just as a saucer would do if you skipped it over water'. The reporter called the craft 'flying saucers'.

Over the following months hundreds of sightings of flying saucers were made. In 1950 a retired US Air Force (USAF) officer named Donald Keyhoe published a book based on his researches into the flying saucers. He described many sightings, making estimates of the size and flying abilities of the saucers. From these Keyhoe deduced that the saucers were not aircraft made by humans and suggested that they were spacecraft carrying aliens who were visiting Earth. Keyhoe stated that the USAF knew far more about the alien spaceships than they were saying in public. Keyhoe's book, *The Flying Saucers are Real*, laid the basis for modern UFO research. His basic ideas are still held by most people who research UFOs, though many new details have been added over the years as more sightings have been made. Most researchers still believe that UFOs are alien spacecraft and that the USAF and other military organisations know far more than they let on.

That is not to say that UFOs really are alien spacecraft. Another suggestion is that they are time machines from Earth's far future, or past. Others think that they may be vehicles used by an advanced Earth-based civilisation, while others link UFOs and the creatures that emerge from them to older accounts of fairies, goblins and elves. Sceptics prefer to explain UFO sightings as hallucinations, misperceived stars, meteors or other ordinary objects – sometimes even as outright lies.

UFO INVESTIGATION ORGANISATIONS

The Mutual UFO Network (MUFON) was founded in 1969 and is based in Colorado. It places great emphasis on scientific study and sends investigators to question witnesses to UFO activity. MUFON produces a monthly newsletter and has about 4,000 members in many countries. Its website can be found at www.mufon.com.

The Aerial Phenomena Enquiry Network (APEN) is a mysterious body run by unknown people. It makes threats against other investigators to try to stop them researching certain sightings, but not others. Some researchers blamed APEN for breaking into offices and for other nefarious activities. APEN began operations in 1974, but by 1990 had apparently ceased their activities.

The Center for Skeptical Inquiry (CSI) is still often called by its former name of Center for Scientific Inquiry of Claims of the Paranormal (CSICOP). It is based in Amherst, New York State, and as its name suggests is composed of people who are highly sceptical of the UFO phenomena. It investigates UFO sightings and other paranormal events and seeks to find natural explanations for the happenings.

The Center for UFO Studies (CUFOS) was founded in 1973 by Dr J. Allen Hynek, a professor of astronomy who had an interest in UFOs. It is based in Chicago and is an international group of scientists, academics, investigators and volunteers dedicated to the continuing examination and analysis of the UFO phenomenon. It aims to promote serious scientific interest in UFOs and to serve as an archive for reports, documents, and publications about the UFO phenomenon. The website can be found at www.cufos.org.

The United States Air Force (USAF) has launched a series of investigations into the UFO phenomenon. The most famous of these was Project Blue Book which ran from 1952 to 1969. Officially these studies concluded that UFOs were not a threat to the security of the USA and so were not the business of the USAF. However, it is known that some details of the studies have been kept secret. Some researchers believe the USAF knows the truth behind the UFOs, but is refusing to make this truth public.

CONTACTEES

The most famous person to have claimed to have spoken to aliens who came to Earth on UFOs was American hamburger salesman George Adamski. He said that he met an alien from Venus on 20 November 1952. Adamski claimed to have travelled to Venus, Jupiter, Saturn and other planets. He said that the aliens were worried for humanity because of the misuse of nuclear power for bombs instead of power stations.

Orfeo Angelucci claimed that on 24 May 1952 he was stopped on his way home from work in California by a UFO. A screen emerged on which were shown a beautiful woman and handsome man, claiming to be aliens. The aliens told Angelucci that they were worried about the future of the Earth and that they would be in touch. Since then Angelucci claimed to have met the aliens several times and to have flown to another planet on a UFO. He died in 1993.

London taxi driver George King claimed that in 1954 he was contacted by an alien from Venus named Aetherius who instructed him to become the representative on Earth of the Interplanetary Parliament. King founded the Aetherius Society to recruit followers and to pass on the messages he received from Aetherius and other aliens. King claimed to have travelled into space several times. On one trip he battled a malevolent dwarf on Mars and on another trip helped to destroy an intelligent meteorite from outside the solar system. King died in 1997, but the Aetherius Society is still going and has a website at www.aetherius.org.

English housewife Cynthia Appleton claimed to have been visited by tall, good looking aliens from the planet Venus three times in 1957/8. She said the aliens told her that UFOs were visiting Earth to extract a mineral from seawater and that the aliens were not hostile. Appleton said that she never saw a UFO, but that the aliens materialised inside her house.

TYPES OF ALIENS

The most regularly sighted type of alien is termed a 'Grey' by researchers. Greys are about 4ft tall with spindly arms and legs and over-large heads. Their eyes are large, black and almond-shaped, but their ears and noses are very small or missing. They have smooth almost shiny skins that are a uniform grey colour. They are sometimes reported to be wearing tight overalls, but are sometimes said to be naked. Greys are said to be able to communicate with humans by way of telepathy. The Greys are the aliens which most often abduct humans, forcing them on board UFOs to undergo medical tests and studies. These tests are sometimes very painful, but the Greys remain indifferent to human suffering. Some witnesses say the Greys are commanded by taller aliens (about 7ft tall) but which are otherwise similar to the Greys.

Encountered less often than Greys are the Insectoids. These aliens have six or eight legs and are dressed in a tight-fitting overall of a black or dark blue colour. They have large eyes and move about with an odd, jerky motion. They often emit clicking noises.

Nordics were met by many witnesses during the 1950s and 1960s, but are now rarely met. They are said to look like humans, but that they are always tall, good looking and perfectly formed. They are often blond and blue-eyed, like stereotypical Swedes or Norwegians, which is how they got their name. Nordics are friendly toward humans, often beckoning witnesses into the UFO for a guided tour of the spacecraft.

Reptoids were first seen in the 1980s and became more common in reports after the year 2000. They are said to be covered in scales, to have reptile-like eyes and sometimes to have webbed feet. They seem to be interested in animals and have been seen abducting cattle, sheep and wildlife.

ABDUCTIONS

In 1961 Betty and Barney Hill were driving home late at night through New Hampshire. They sighted a UFO and their car engine died. They restarted the engine when the UFO left and drove home, but noticed that they were much later than they should have been. Under hypnosis they recalled that a group of 5ft-tall aliens dressed in black uniforms had emerged from the UFO and forced them on board. Once on the UFO, the Hills were subjected to a series of medical tests. The aliens were fascinated by Barney's false teeth. Betty asked the aliens where they were from and was shown a star map. The Hills were then led back to their car and had their memories wiped by the aliens. Betty drew a copy of the star map, which was identified by an astronomer as being of the system Zeta Reticuli. The

Hills were the first people to report having been abducted in this way, but since then hundreds of people have claimed a similar experience.

The Allagash Abductions of 26 August 1976 involved four students: Charlie Foltz, Chuck Rak and Jim and Jack Weiner. While fishing at East Lake, Massachusetts, the four men saw a UFO, but later could not remember what had happened. Under hypnosis the men later recalled a broadly similar series of events to the Hills. They were transported into the UFO along a beam of light, forced to undress and subjected to a series of medical tests that involved probes collecting samples of blood, saliva, skin and urine. The men were then ordered to dress and were transported back to their camp where their memories were wiped. The four men later passed a lie detector test when questioned about the abduction.

BIZARRE ENCOUNTERS

On 16 October 1957 Argentinian farmer Antonio Boas found a UFO in a field on his farm. He was pounced on by short, hairy aliens who hauled him on board the UFO and conducted a series of medical tests on him. The encounter took a turn for the bizarre when the aliens introduced him to a beautiful and apparently human woman with whom Boas had sex. Boas was then given his clothes and thrown off the UFO. He later suffered attacks of severe nausea.

In December 1967 Danish UFO researcher Hans Lauritzen sighted a pair of yellow UFOs near his home. He fell into a trance for an hour, and when he awoke found that he had been cured of a liver infection that had been making him very ill. He recalled communicating via telepathy with aliens in the UFOs. They had told him that he was very important to mankind, but did not specify how.

DANGEROUS ALIENS

Venezuelan farm workers Gustavo Gonzalez and Jose Ponce set off before dawn on 28 November 1954 to walk to market near Caracas. They saw a UFO and were then attacked by three hairy creatures that looked like upright walking apes about 4ft tall. Ponce fled to a nearby police station while Gonzalez fought back with his knife. Gonzalez was suddenly paralysed by a beam of light shot at him from a tube-like object held by one of the creatures. The hairy beings then climbed into the UFO and flew off before police could arrive.

On 21 August 1955 the farm belonging to the Sutton family near Hopkinsville, Kentucky, was attacked by a group of aliens who are presumed to have emerged from a UFO sighted earlier that day. The aliens were described as being 3ft tall with large heads, pointed ears and enormous eyes, but tiny noses and mouths. Their long, thin arms ended with three fingers each equipped with a savage claw. When the first creature appeared it ran towards the house with its claws raised over its head. Bill Sutton shot it with his rifle. Although the creature fled it did not seem to have been injured. For the next hour the creatures tried several times to get into the house, each time being driven off by gunfire. When the aliens left, the Suttons raced into town in their car to alert the police.

MEN IN BLACK

Some people who have seen UFOs report that they are later visited by sinister men dressed in black who try to threaten them into keeping quiet about what they have seen. On 11 September 1976 UFO researcher Herbert Hopkins was visited by a bald man dressed in a black suit and black hat. The man told Hopkins to stop investigating a recent UFO sighting and threatened to kill him if he did not comply. The stranger then began slur his words and announced, 'My energy is running low. I must leave.' The man in black walked out of the house, leaving a mystified and worried Hopkins.

In 1952 Italian fisherman Carlo Rossi saw a UFO near his home in San Pietro a Vico. A few days later he was approached by a tall man in a dark blue suit who spoke in a strong Germanic accent. The man looked menacing in a strange way. He asked Rossi if he had seen any unusual flying objects recently. Rossi said that he had not. The stranger then left.

In 1954 UFO researcher Albert Bender woke up to find three men standing in his bedroom. They were dressed in black suits and black hats. The three men spoke to Bender in foreign accents instructing him to stop investigating UFOs. Something about the men terrified Bender, who promptly ceased his work.

In July 1967 Robert Richardson of Toledo, Ohio, saw a UFO on his way home from work. Three days later two men in dark suits arrived in an old-fashioned black car. They questioned Richardson about his sighting, then left. A week later two different men arrived, again in dark suits but this time speaking in foreign accents. They told Richardson to forget everything he had seen, 'If you want your wife to stay as pretty as she is.' Then they left.

In 1976 Mexican Carlos de los Santos was walking home after giving a radio interview about a UFO he had seen a few weeks earlier when two large black cars pulled up beside him. Two men got out of one of the cars and approached him. They were dressed in dark suits and hats. One of the men blocked the pavement and jabbed his finger at Santos.

'If you value your life,' the man said in a foreign accent, 'don't talk any more about your sighting.' The two men then got back in their car and both vehicles roared off.

CLOSE ENCOUNTERS OF THE FIRST KIND

A close encounter of the first kind is when a person sees a UFO at such close quarters that there is no possibility that they could be mistaken in what they are seeing. The UFO could not, for instance, be a normal aircraft or a star seen under unusual atmospheric conditions.

At Parshall, North Dakota, on 27 October 1967 at 3 a.m. a policeman was patrolling in his car when he saw a brightly lit object hovering about 100ft above the ground. It was almost spherical and bobbed slightly. The object then began moving, gathering speed as it did so but maintaining its undulating motion. After a final bounce the object accelerated sharply and shot upwards out of sight at tremendous speed.

Four nurses were driving to work at 7.40 p.m. on 11 January 1966 outside Myerstown, Pennsylvania, when they saw a flying object. It was about 100yds away and was shaped like two saucers placed rim to rim. It was glowing as if it was made of frosted glass and had a bright light within it. It hovered, wobbling slightly for about five minutes, then abruptly flew off at tremendous speed.

Just outside the village of Snopousov in Czechoslovakia on 1 July 1966 Mrs Vlasta Rosenauerova and her two children saw two red objects flying towards her house at 9 p.m. As the objects approached she saw that they were round with domes on top. The objects began to descend in a spiralling motion, then stopped. They hovered for about five minutes, then moved off to the east, flying low over a nearby wood.

CLOSE ENCOUNTERS OF THE SECOND KIND

A close encounter of the second kind occurs when a UFO leaves solid traces behind to show that it had really existed.

At Cochrane, Wisconsin, on 3 April 1968 a schoolteacher was driving home at 8 p.m. when she saw a crescent-shaped object that was pulsating with an internal red light fly down to hover over the road ahead. As she got closer her car's lights went out and the engine failed. The object then moved to be directly over her car, where it hovered. She tried to restart the car, but couldn't. The object then glided away toward some nearby railway tracks. When the object had gone the teacher was able to start her car normally and drove home.

On 9 November 1979 forestry worker Robert Taylor was walking through a forest plantation looking for some wayward sheep. Entering a clearing he found himself facing a dark, domed object about 20ft across with a raised rim around its edge. It was hovering just above the ground in utter silence. Two small globes then raced across the clearing toward Taylor. Each had a series of spikes protruding from it; these attached themselves to Taylor's clothing and pulled him over, dragging him toward the domed object and tearing his trousers. A terrific stench of burning rubber filled the air. Taylor broke free, then fainted. When he came round the objects had gone. He staggered back to his truck and radioed for help. When the police arrived they found marks on the ground as if some very heavy object had rested there.

CLOSE ENCOUNTERS OF THE THIRD KIND

A close encounter of the third kind takes place when a person sees a UFO at close range and sees creatures emerge from it.

On 12 September 1952 three boys saw what they thought was a meteor crash into woods near their homes in Flatwoods, West Virginia. They went to investigate with an adult neighbour, Mrs Kathleen May. They found a glowing ball about the size of a house hovering in a clearing in the woods. Nearby stood a figure about 15ft tall who was wrapped in a billowing black cloak. When the figure began moving toward them, the witnesses fled. The next day strange marks were found in the ground of the clearing and a terrible stench filled the air.

In 1959 Father William Gill was at work on his remote mission station in New Guinea when a large disc-shaped object came down through the clouds and hovered overhead. Gill and his workers watched as four apparently human figures appeared on a deck-like area and carried out what appeared to be maintenance tasks on the flying craft. Gill waved, and one of the human figures waved back. The object remained in sight for over an hour, then flew off. At the time Gill thought the flying disc was an aircraft from a nearby USAF base and only later did he learn that the USAF had no such craft in its possession.

On 24 April 1964 a New Mexico policeman was sent to investigate an apparent explosion in the desert near Socorro. He found an oval, white object standing on legs and accompanied by two humanoid figures about 4ft tall and dressed in white overalls. The two figures climbed into the craft, which took off with a roar and flew off at high speed.

In 1965 French farmer Maurice Masse was working his fields of lavender when he saw what he thought were two young boys pulling up plants. Masse went to confront the 'boys' only to find that they were humanoids in tight green overalls. The figures were about 4ft tall and had very large, smooth, hairless heads. One of the figures pointed a tube at him and a flash of light paralysed Masse. The figures then climbed into a round object, which flew off at speed.

CRASH RETRIEVALS

In 1950 rumours spread that a UFO had crashed at Aztec, New Mexico. It was said that the crew of 16 aliens had died in the crash and that the wreck had been impounded by the USAF.

A few months later two men named Silas Newton and Leo GeBauer launched a company to exploit alien technology that they said they had stolen from the crashed spacecraft. They were later convicted of fraud as they had no alien technology in their possession. It was never clear if they had started the rumour or if they had exploited a genuine story.

In October 1947 newspapers carried unconfirmed reports that a UFO had crashed in the Cave Creek area of Paradise Valley, Arizona. Allegedly a saucer about 36ft in diameter came down in the desert. There were two alien bodies recovered from this craft, which had been smashed open by the impact. One body was sitting upright at the controls, the second was slumped halfway out of a hatchway.

On 7 July 1948 a UFO was seen flying over Albuquerque at very high speed. Later that day personnel from nearby Carswell air base were turned out to cordon off and mount armed guard over an area of barren semi-desert. The men were told that nobody was allowed access to the area, and that they were not allowed inside the perimeter that they were guarding either. The men guarding the perimeter of the area became convinced that they were protecting a crashed flying saucer. None of those willing to talk on the record after the event had actually seen the saucer, but they were convinced that at least one of their comrades had done.

A flight of six Norwegian military jets was on patrol over the Arctic Hinlopen Straits north of the Norwegian mainland in June 1952. Quite suddenly their radios were swamped by static as they crossed the coast of the island of Spitsbergen. The flight commander, Captain Olaf Larsen, ordered his formation to circle while he tried to reach base on his radio. He failed, but far below him he caught the glint of sun sparkling off metal. Going down to investigate, Larsen saw what he took to be a large, circular metal object embedded in the snow of the remote frozen island. The craft was said to be around 150ft in diameter and bore abstract symbols of some kind. He reported the sighting to more senior officers, but never heard anything more about the incident.

In July 1947 the local newspaper and radio station at Roswell, New Mexico, carried reports that a local rancher had found a crashed flying saucer on his land. The USAF was alerted and military teams moved in to collect the wreckage. The USAF later announced that the crashed craft was actually a weather balloon. In 1980s UFO researchers reinvestigated the incident and found that no weather balloon had been in the area at the time. They also found witnesses who described finding a crashed aircraft like nothing made on Earth, and dead bodies and wreckage with bizarre properties. A subsequent USAF investigation found that the original announcement of a weather balloon had been invented to cover up the crash of an experimental craft, but many researchers remain convinced that it was a UFO that crashed at Roswell.

2

BIGFOOT & MAN-APES

Stories, tales and rumours filter out of remote forested regions that there exists a human-like ape which is totally unknown to science, but which is a very real animal. There is not just one such creature said to be stalking the Earth, there are several: Bigfoot, Yeti, Almá, Didi, Orang Pendek, Skunk Ape, Yowie and others. There have been hundreds of sightings of these creatures over the years, but no firm evidence that would convince the scientific world that the things exist.

Many scientists simply refuse to believe that any animal so large could continue to survive into the modern world without the scientific establishment being aware of it. However, the fact that large creatures can survive undetected by the establishment is well known. Take, for instance, the saola. For years villagers in the Annamite Hills of Vietnam had been telling outsiders that there was a rare type of forest antelope living in the jungles near their villages. It was called the saola. Nobody took the stories very seriously. Even during the height of the Vietnam War, when the whole country was filled with foreign soldiers, nobody reported seeing one of these elusive creatures. The scientific establishment simply discounted the tales as being examples of mistaken identity, or of invented folklore.

Then in 1992 one villager gave a pair of horns that he said came from the forest antelope to a European zoologist. The zoologist was puzzled. He did not recognise the horns at all. With solid evidence to hand the scientists now took the stories seriously, using them to build up a picture of a bovid mammal that lived in the Annamite Hills, ate the leaves of forest shrubs and moved in small groups. They set off to find the creature, armed with all the paraphernalia of a high-tech modern scientific investigation. It did not take them long to find the animal. Not only did it turn out to be a new species of mammal, but it belonged to a previously unknown genus and no scientist was quite sure how it was related to any other type of antelope.

That such a creature as an antelope could survive in a remote region entirely unknown to science came as something of a surprise, but it is not alone. New species of mammal are being discovered nearly every year.

For the scientific establishment to recognise a type of animal as officially existing they generally demand an example, either living or dead, to be delivered to a museum or specialist zoologist. Alternatively, if a respected zoologist were to see such a creature at close quarters, but be unable to bring a specimen back, it would probably lead to a detailed search such as that which uncovered the saola.

Meanwhile, the study of unrecognised animals is known as cryptozoology – meaning 'the study of hidden animals' – while the unrecognised creatures themselves are termed cryptids – meaning 'hidden ones'. Some cryptozoologists have spent years searching for firm evidence that a cryptid does exist. Some have collected impressive archives of evidence. But in general we have only eyewitness accounts and a few photographs or snatches of film to provide evidence that such mysterious man-apes do exist.

THE BIGFOOT OR SASQUATCH

Living in the more remote forested regions of North America there is said to be a huge ape that walks upright like a human. The Bigfoot or Sasquatch is said to stand up to 7 or 8ft tall. It is reportedly broader and more muscular than a human, having a build more like that of a gorilla. The creature is covered in short, reddish-brown or black hair, with only the face and the palms and soles of the feet left bare. In past centuries it was seen in many different parts of the continent, but is now encountered only in the western and northern forests. Presumably the spread of European-style civilisation has pushed the Sasquatch out of its former homeland. Bigfoot first hit the headlines outside of its usual range in 1958 when a crew of workmen building a road were so shocked by the visit of a Bigfoot that they stopped work on the project. Since then the subject has been studied more intensively.

EARLY BIGFOOT SIGHTINGS

In August 1818 a man out walking in the woods near Ellisburgh, New York State, saw a 'wild man' emerge into a clearing. The figure was described as being basically human, but covered in hair and having large feet. As soon as it saw the witness, the creature ran off back into the trees.

A small hairy ape, perhaps a young Bigfoot, was seen in Pennsylvania in 1834. A man out picking wild berries saw the ape walking upright toward him. As soon as the ape saw the witness it gave a loud whistling call and fled. The creature was said to be about the height of a seven-year-old boy, but covered in short black hair.

A herd of cattle in Green County, Kentucky, began milling about as if frightened so the farmer went to see if a wolf or other wild animal was in the area. He found himself confronted by, 'An animal bearing the unmistakeable likeness of humanity, of gigantic stature, the body being covered with hair.' Both man and Bigfoot turned and fled from each other.

In 1869 a hunter in California found his camp disturbed. He sat up over the camp next day to try to catch the intruder. He watched as a hairy man about 5ft tall arrived in the camp. The intruder gave a loud, piercing whistle. It then picked up a stick from the campfire and swung it around a few times. A similar female creature then arrived, and the two walked off into the forest.

DANGEROUS BIGFOOT

In the 1860s a hunter named Bauman was trapping fur in Montana. When he and his companion came back to camp one day they found that the tent had been smashed, the equipment scattered and their food stores ripped open and much of it eaten. The only clues were gigantic footprints of naked, apparently human feet. The men decided to leave the area. Bauman went out to collect the traps, but when he came back he found his companion lying dead with a broken neck and fresh giant footprints around the camp. Bauman fled.

In 1943 prospector John McQuire staggered into Ruby, Alaska. He said that he had been attacked by a large, hairy 'bushman', but that his dogs had chased the creature away. McQuire was badly injured and died a few days later.

KIDNAPPED BY BIGFOOT

In 1871 a seventeen-year-old Amerindian woman went missing from her home in the Harrison River valley of British Columbia. She returned a few months later, sick and malnourished. She told her family that she had been grabbed by a male Bigfoot and carried away deep into the forests. She had been forced to stay in a cave by the Bigfoot, which was joined by other Bigfoot who seemed to be a family group. She was fed by them, but when she fell sick they seemed to lose interest in her and she escaped.

In 1924 hunter Albert Ostman was camping at Toba Inlet, British Columbia. He was awoken when his sleeping bag was lifted up and carried off, with him still in it, by unseen hands. Ostman was carried for some hours before being dropped. Emerging from his sleeping bag, Ostman saw he was in a narrow ravine together with four Bigfoots: an adult couple and two young. The older male blocked Ostman's exit when he tried to leave the ravine. After seven days, Ostman tricked the large male Bigfoot into trying some snuff. While the Bigfoot retched, Ostman fled. He was chased by the adult female, but fired a shot over her head which made her stop.

In 1928 a native trapper, Muchalat Harry, was trapped by a group of twenty Bigfoots on Vancouver Island. The Bigfoots were not violent, but stopped all his attempts to move off. They seemed fascinated by his clothes, which they kept plucking at. After some hours they lost interest and Harry fled.

HUNGRY BIGFOOT

In September 1941 Mrs Jean Chapman saw a Bigfoot walking toward her wooden house near Ruby Creek in British Columbia. The Bigfoot was over 7ft tall and covered in yellowish-brown hair. She grabbed her children and fled. When Mr Chapman came home from work he found that the storeroom door had been smashed and a barrel of salted fish dragged out and opened. The Bigfoot had eaten several fish, then left again.

North America's Sasquatch, or Bigfoot, is reported as walking and running upright like a human, but to stand about 8ft tall. The creature is reportedly covered in dense fur, and emits yelping and whistling sounds.

In October 1955 hunter William Roe was looking for bear on Mica Mountain, British Columbia. He saw a Bigfoot over 6ft tall feeding on berries from a bush and stopped to watch it. The creature was covered in dark brown, silver-tipped fur and was very broad and muscular, weighing around 300lbs. The creature began eating leaves, then sensed Roe and turned to look at him. The creature made a noise like a horse whinny, then walked off. Roe aimed his rifle, but then decided the creature was too much like a human to shoot and let it leave.

Gary Joanis shot a deer at Wanoga Butte, Oregon, in October 1957. As soon as the deer had dropped, a 7ft-tall Bigfoot emerged from nearly bushes, picked it up and gave a loud whistling call. The Bigfoot tucked the deer under its arm and calmly walked off.

BIGFOOT ON CAMERA

Most film or video footage that appears to show a Bigfoot has been shown to be faked – usually it is footage of a man in a monkey suit. However, a few pieces of film have not been proved to be hoaxes.

The classic Bigfoot movie was shot on 20 October 1967 by two rodeo riders, Roger Patterson and Bob Gimlin. The two men were looking for Bigfoot tracks seen a few days earlier. As they rode around a bend in a valley, they sighted a female Bigfoot about 50ft in front of them. Patterson grabbed a cine camera from his saddlebags and leapt from his horse to film the creature as it walked off into nearby woodland. Gimlin kept Patterson covered with a rifle. As the creature walked off it turned to look at Patterson providing the most often printed image of a Bigfoot.

In 1994 former patrolman Paul Freeman was videoing a line of Bigfoot tracks when he heard bushes moving. He lifted the camera and managed to shoot several seconds of film as a Bigfoot walked past some bushes, paused to stare at Freeman and then walked off into dense forest. As it walks off, the Bigfoot bends down to pick something up, perhaps a baby.

The Redwoods Footage of a Bigfoot was shot in 1995 by a TV crew of Waterland Productions who were returning from a filming assignment. As they drove through some forests a Bigfoot was seen crossing the road ahead of them in the headlights of their vehicle. One man grabbed the TV camera and shot a few seconds of video as the creature walked off into the woods.

In 1996 Lori Pate shot a video of a Bigfoot walking across a forest meadow near Copaka Lake, Washington. The Bigfoot is shown running across the grass, behind a grassy knoll and into tree cover.

TWENTY-FIRST CENTURY BIGFOOT

Forestry Manager, David Mills, was on the Kitsap Peninsula of Washington State on 29 June 2000 when he heard a heavy thumping noise. Looking round he saw a Bigfoot pounding on a tree with a rock. Beyond the Bigfoot was a bear with a cub. The bear snarled angrily and advanced on the Bigfoot. Not having a gun, Mills backed away then ran off as the sounds of the two giant beasts confronting each other grew louder.

A foul stench surprised Dr Johnson at the Oregon Caves on 1 July 2000. He looked around and saw a Bigfoot about 60ft away. It looked at him, then walked off into trees.

Mrs Linda Boydson was driving through woodland near Multnomah in Oregon when she came around a corner to see a Bigfoot in the middle of the road. She slammed on her brakes, stopping just a few feet from the creature. She estimated the animal was about 9ft tall and covered in brown fur. It looked skinny and sick. The Bigfoot casually ambled off to be lost in the trees.

A Bigfoot invaded a trailer park on 22 February 2004 when one strolled into Fort Berthold in North Dakota. It was startled when a group of children began screaming and ran away.

At 1 a.m. on 6 June 2004 Gus Jules and Marion Sheldon were driving along the Alaska Highway in the Yukon when they saw what they thought was a man in a coat crouched by the side of the road. They pulled over and called out to see if the man needed any help. The figure then stood up to show itself to be a 7ft-tall Bigfoot which looked at them, then began to walk toward them. Jules and Sheldon drove off at speed.

THE SKUNK APE

The Skunk Ape got its name because of the hideous stench that is reported by many witnesses. It is reported to live in forests and swamps in Florida and neighbouring states. This cryptid is said to look rather like an orangutan and is definitely more like an ape than like a human. The footprints that it leaves have a large gap between the big toe and the other toes, again like an ape. This would indicate that it uses it feet to grip branches as it climbs in trees.

In 1900 a 'wild man' was reported to be living on an island in the Mississippi River in Missouri. A police patrol captured the animal, which they identified as being an orangutan. They passed it on to a circus owner who wanted it.

In 1960 Sheriff T. Lochart and Deputy James Johnson were following up a report of a gorilla on the loose when they found tracks that, they reported, looked like they had been made by a man walking on his hands. With a big toe separated from the others, a Skunk Ape track would look like hand prints.

In February 1970 Nathan Russell was walking through woodland near Central City, Arkansas, when he saw something in a tree. The creature jumped down and stood on its hind legs with long arms swinging in front of it. It was about 5ft 8in tall and covered in long brown hair. Russell ran, and the creature gave chase. When Russell reached the front porch of a house, the creature gave up the chase and vanished into the woods.

A bunch of bananas was put out to feed a Skunk Ape by the groundsman of Delray Beach Golf Course in Florida in February 1977. The man had seen the Skunk Ape drinking from a pond on the golf course the night before and he thought the animal might be hungry. The bananas were gone a short time later.

Baptist Minister S.L. Whatley was cutting firewood near his home at Ocala, Florida, when he saw an ape-like creature watching him from about 300yds distance. The creature was covered in dark fur and had a chocolate-coloured face free of hair. The arms were long and hung down loosely. Whatley picked up an axe intending to tackle the creature, but it scampered off.

In the autumn of 2000 a woman living near Myakka in Florida heard strange 'woomp' noises from outside her house one evening. She went outside and saw a Skunk Ape hiding among some bushes. She grabbed a camera and took two photos. These seem to show an orangutan-like creature

ORANG PENDEK

Living in the densest jungles of Sumatra, the Orang Pendek is said to be far more like a human than an ape. It stands upright on its hind legs and reaches a height of about 3 or 4ft. It is covered in short, brown or black fur and some – perhaps males – have a mane of longer hair over their head and shoulders. It has no tail and the arms are in proportion to those of humans, not

The Orang Pendek of Sumatra is invariably described as being a slender, ape-like creature that walks upright more easily than other apes. The fur is short and dark grey or black in colour.

long like those of apes. These creatures have been reported to communicate with each other in a chattering noise that sounds like language more than it does like an animal call. The Orang Pendek has been seen eating fruit, leaves, shoots, worms, shellfish and even snakes. Most sightings have been made by local people, who view the Orang Pendek as a perfectly normal creature like others in the jungles. A few Europeans have seen an Orang Pendek and have written down what they witnessed.

In 1910 L. Westenek was surpervising a team of log cutters in forest near Barissan. One day a team of men came out of the forest early and announced that they would do no more work in the area but demanded that they be moved to another location. The men were not native to the forests and were obviously scared by something. They told Westenek that they had been startled by a creature that looked like a small man, but was covered in hair. It had walked like a man and come to within 15yds of them before they ran.

On 10 July 1916 Edward Jacobson came across an Orang Pendek in the forests on the Bocket Kaba mountain. The creature was engrossed in pulling apart a rotten log looking for grubs and insects. Jacobson was behind the creature and he crept forwards as quietly as he could. He had got to within just 20yds of the creature when it suddenly turned around to look at him and then ran off. Up to this point Jacobson had thought he was dealing with an orangutan and was most surprised when it ran off like a human. The footprints the creature left behind were similar to those of a ten-year-old child, but a bit wider than expected.

In 1923 a Mr van Herwaarden was travelling through the forest near Pangkalan Balai when he saw a creature on a branch of a tree. He started to climb the tree, but found he could not get up it, so he walked to stand directly under the creature, which had been watching him. He said that the face of the animal had a nose and eyes like a human's but was rather pointed at the chin and wide across the cheeks. The creature made a 'hu-hu' call. When this was answered from among undergrowth nearby, the creature leapt down from the branch and ran off in that direction.

During the 1990s British naturalist Debbie Martyr made a study of the Orang Pendek. She collected hair samples that have been analysed. They are similar to ape hair, but cannot be identified as being from any known species. Martyr claims to have seen an Orang Pendek herself.

YETI

The Yeti is said to be a large, gorilla-like ape that lives in the Himalayan Mountains. Although the footprints of this creature have been reported in the high mountain snows, it is thought to live in the forested valleys. It may cross the snows to travel from one valley to another. It is said to live across a wide area and is known by various names in different languages. The Sherpa people call the creature the 'metoh-kangmi' which was translated in the 1920s to mean 'abominable snowman'. The name Yeti comes from the Nepalese language.

In 1832 Brian Hodgson was trekking in Nepal when he saw what he described as a large orangutan. The creature fled as soon as it saw Hodgson.

In 1925 Greek photographer N. Tombazi was travelling near Zemu when he saw an upright figure covered in hair about 300yds away. It seemed to be pulling shoots from rhododendron bushes. He later visited the bushes and found footprints that looked similar to those of a human that were 8in long and 4in wide.

In 1910 William Knight was in forests near Gangtok when a figure emerged from undergrowth about 20yds away. The figure was about 6ft tall and a yellowish-brown colour.

On 8 November 1951 British climbers Eric Shipton and Michael Ward were on the southern slopes of Menlungtse when they found a trail of what looked like enormous human footprints. They followed the tracks for more than a mile before they vanished on rocky ground. The prints showed that the big toe was separated from the others by a gap – like an ape's foot. Each print was about 12in long. The stride length indicated that if they were made by a creature walking on two legs like a human then the creature had been about 7ft tall. Shipton took two photos: one of the trail and one of an individual footprint. The photos caused a sensation and made the Yeti world-famous.

On 18 April 1952 French climbers René Dittert and André Roch had to turn

The Yeti of the Himalayas is usually described as being ape-like, though witnesses often report it standing and walking upright. It is described as being thickset and muscular, but otherwise of being roughly human in size.

back from a climb on the lower slopes of Mount Everest when a thick fog came down. They tried again next day and found that their returning prints of the day before were overlaid by huge footprints like those of a shoeless man. They concluded that they had been followed in the fog by three Yetis.

In September 1953 a Sherpa named Pasang Nyima was sitting watching his yak herd when a Yeti came down the grassy slope. It was about 5ft tall and covered in brown hair that was longer on its head and shoulders than elsewhere. There was little fur below the knees. The creature stopped now and then to poke under rocks as if looking for grubs or worms. When it saw Nyima the Yeti gave a high-pitched yelp and ran off into some nearby woodland.

In 1970 British climber Don Whillans saw a large creature near his camp in the moonlight. It looked like an ape and moved both on all fours and upright. He later found human-like footprints in the area in which he had seen the creature.

American TV presenter Joshua Gates was filming in the Himalayas in December 2007 when he came across a Yeti track. He made plaster casts of the footprints, which were 13in long and 9in across. The prints were roughly human in shape, but had an oddly-shaped big toe.

THE ALMAS

The mountains of Central Asia, especially the Altai and Pamir ranges, are said to be home to a type of man-ape called the Almas. The Almas are reported to be almost human in appearance, apart from a covering of dense fur all over their bodies. The face is hairless and the eyebrows project forward in a ridge of bone. The creatures are said to walk with a stooping gait, with the feet splayed inward. The creatures are said to eat mostly, or exclusively, plant foods and for some unknown reason are often encountered close to herds of wild goats. Some researchers believe they may be a species of human such as Homo erectus or Neanderthal man.

Bavarian nobleman Hans Schiltberger travelled to Mongolia in the 1420s. He reported seeing two 'wild people' being kept in a Mongolian zoo. He described them as being like humans, but covered in dense fur.

Russian scientist Badzare Baradyine was travelling near Alachan in April 1906 when he saw a human-like figure standing on a nearby hill watching his caravan passing by. The strange figure was covered in fur which was a reddish-brown colour and tightly curled.

In 1925 General Mikhail Topilski of the Communist Red Army was hunting anti-Communist rebels in the Pamir region. During a fight they accidentally killed an adult male Almas. The body was very similar to that of a man, about 5ft 6in tall, but it was covered in dense hair that was longer on the shoulders and chest than elsewhere. The lower arms and lower legs had less hair, while the hands and feet were hairless. The forehead sloped

The Almas of the mountainous regions of southern Mongolia and eastern Russia are usually described as being rather more human in appearance and habits than are other humanoid cryptids. There are several reports of the Almas using tools and it has been speculated that they may be isolated survivors of the Neanderthal or Homo erectus forms of humans.

back from a thick bone ridge over the eyes. The teeth were rather large, but otherwise like those of a human.

In 1963 Russian scientist Ivan Ivlov was travelling through the Altai Mountains when he sighted three human-like figures about half a mile away. He watched the figures through binoculars and saw that they were covered in fur like apes. The figures seemed to be an adult male, a female and a child. The local man with Ivlov said that the Almas usually stayed away from humans, but were not rare.

In 1980 Russian student Nina Grineva was part of a scientific field expedition in the Pamirs when she came face to face with an Almas in a forest. The creature looked like a tall, muscular man covered in dark, silver-tipped fur. Nina had in her pocket a small cuddly toy with a squeak. She held it out and the Almas seemed interested in it. When she squeezed it to make a squeak, the Almas looked surprised and then ran off out of sight.

THE YOWIE

The Yowie is said to be a large ape that walks upright and is covered in dense fur. It is supposed to live in the forested hills of eastern Australia, but has been seen in other areas of the continent. Aborigine legends often include accounts of wild men, hairy men or devil men, but it is not clear if these are accounts of real creatures or mythical monsters.

Australia's Yowie has been seen preying on kangaroos, wombats and other animals. It is often said to have clawed hands and fang-like teeth, though not all witnesses report these features.

In 1861 Mr B. Rixon, who lived near the Cordeaux River in New South Wales, reported meeting an ape in the bush country.

In 1865 shepherd George Long was camped out near Naseby, New South Wales, when his sheepdogs began growling at something. Long saw what looked like a man about 7ft tall in the darkness under a tree. He fired his gun, and the man-like figure ran off. Next morning Long went to investigate with one of his Aboriginal herders. The Aborigine took one look at the tracks, declared them to be of a 'dibbil dibbil' and refused to go any further saying that the giant was dangerous.

In February 1932 William Nuttall was riding home after dark to his home near Eurobin in Victoria. He was suddenly attacked by a snarling animal which sprang up and caused the horse to bolt, throwing Nuttall to the ground. Nuttall ran, leaping over a wire fence. The creature stopped on the far side of the fence, then ran off into the darkness. Nuttall said the creature was about the same size as himself, but covered in hair and that it revealed four very long, sharp teeth when it snarled. He thought it might have been a type of ape.

In January 1974 Michael Allison and his two brothers were driving home late one night to Whiporie in New South Wales. As they came around a corner they saw what looked like a gorilla standing by the side of the road. The creature was caught in their headlights for a couple of seconds, then moved off.

On 25 September 2004 Dean Grebo was camping in Bungonia Gorge, New South Wales. Late in the evening he heard a strange screeching sound from the darkness. He switched on his torch and saw about 20yds away what he said looked like a monkey standing on its hind legs and about 4ft tall. It had a dead possum in its hands. The creature screamed loudly, bared its teeth and ran off into the darkness.

3

GHOSTS & HAUNTINGS

Ghosts can be a surprisingly varied group of paranormal entities. There are terrifying headless knights stomping about medieval castles and there are white ladies lurking by roadsides to spook unwary motorists; but there are also ghosts dressed in perfectly normal everyday clothes who do nobody any harm and seem almost incapable of scaring anyone. There are phantoms that throw furniture about, smash windows, hurl stones and generally make a complete nuisance of themselves, and there are quiet spectres who just sit quietly and let the world go by. In fact what are loosely referred to as ghosts and hauntings cover a wide range of paranormal activity. It is very likely that one type of haunting may have nothing to do with another. The various categories of ghost may be caused by quite different types of paranormal entity or energy. Some investigators would object to the term 'ghost' being used at all as the various phenomena are so varied that they should not be lumped together.

What might be termed a classic ghost is an apparition in the form of a person or persons who has died some time earlier. Such ghosts are not, contrary to the spectres shown in films, semi-transparent nor do they often float through the air. When encountered they appear to be quite solid and are sometimes at first mistaken for a real person. These classic ghosts typically frequent a place that the person who they represent knew and was familiar with when alive. They seem to repeat time and again a particular action such as walking down a staircase or staring out of a window. They will sometimes behave in a very odd way, such as walking through solid walls or floating in mid-air. When investigations are possible it usually turns out that when the person was alive a door existed in the wall or that the floor level was higher. These ghosts rarely, if ever, interact with the human witness. It is as if they are operating on a quite different plane from ourselves.

Rather different are what might be termed presence entities. These ghosts are hardly ever seen, but they make their presence felt in the form of a very strong atmosphere. A person entering a room will be aware that, say, a kindly old lady is sitting in the corner or that an angry young woman is peering through a window even though nothing is visible. In a few exceptional instances a presence entity can interact with its surroundings. It may resent having furniture or other objects placed where it habitually manifests itself and will push these away or move them to one side. Attempts to speak to such manifestations are usually fruitless – at best the presence will suddenly go away or intensify its emotional impact if spoken to.

Perfectly capable of speaking to witnesses are the crisis apparitions that appear when a person is undergoing a crisis of some kind. Typically a crisis apparition will appear when a person is dying or suffers a sudden serious injury. An apparition of that person will then appear in front of a friend or relative. Such apparitions are perfectly solid and may be mistaken for the real person. They very rarely pass on a message about what is happening to their real selves, but engage in everyday conversation about the weather or mutual acquaintances – if they speak at all.

There are other types of ghosts and the various researchers prefer different methods of classifying the phantoms and spectres that are reported by witnesses. What all ghosts have in common is an ability to manifest themselves spontaneously and unexpectedly. This makes them difficult to study as a researcher might sit in a haunted room for hours on end, only for the ghost to appear when he pops out to make a cup of tea.

AT THE MOMENT OF DEATH

On 7 December 1918 Lt Larkin of the British RAF was relaxing in his room at RAF Scampton. He heard footsteps in the corridor and his room-mate Lt M'Connel opened the door.

'Hello,' said Larkin, 'back already?'.

'Yes,' replied M'Connel, 'I had a good trip.' Then M'Connel shut the door. In fact M'Connel had not had a good trip, but had crashed his aircraft in fog and died instantly – at the very moment that Larkin saw him enter their room.

Novelist Anna Maria Porter was relaxing in her house in Esher in 1812 when she saw a friend who lived a mile away enter the room. The man stood for a moment in silence, appearing to be upset or anxious, then he left again. Porter sent a servant to chase after the man, but he could not be seen. The servant then ran to the man's house to see if anything was wrong only to be told that the man had suffered a sudden seizure and fallen down dead barely an hour earlier, which would have been about the time Porter had seen him in her house.

On 3 January 1856 Mrs Mary Collyer was resting in her room when she saw her son Joseph enter. He was supposed to have been abroad on business, so Mrs Collyer was very surprised. Joseph was dressed in a nightshirt. He looked at his mother sadly, then vanished into thin air. Ten days later a telegram arrived to say that Joseph had been killed in a shipwreck – on 3 January.

In August 1926 Irish landowner Mrs Godley went with her assistant Miss Goldsmith, to visit an estate worker named Robert Bowes who had been taken ill. After the visit the two women were travelling home in a pony and trap when they both saw Bowes punting a boat across a lake. They were surprised as Bowes had been very ill. A short time after they got home the two ladies received a message to say that Bowes had died about twenty minutes after they left – which was when they had seen his apparition on the lake.

One day in 1828 a Mrs Edden of Haddenham, Buckinghamshire, suddenly fainted just outside the parish church. She recovered her senses to tell the anxious villagers that she had just seen a phantom of her husband. Not only did the ghost tell her that he had been murdered, but also named his killers. Mr Edden was out that day collecting rents from local farmers. A man set out to track him down and found his dead body by the roadside. The magistrates were alerted and the alleged culprits arrested. They were found to have Mr Edden's purse full of coins in their possession and, after the briefest of trials, were hanged. The sighting of the apparition was not given in evidence at the trial.

CHURCH GHOSTS

In Bristol, All Saints' Church harbours a phantom monk. When orders came from King Henry VIII to close down the monastery of which this church was a part, the monks buried their holy treasures. When one monk remonstrated with the angry soldiers for their supposed impiety, he was struck so hard that he fell back and smashed his head on the pavement. He died soon after, and his ghost began to walk. It is generally supposed that the ghost is guarding the great treasure hidden thereabouts. Whether he is trying to lead people to it, or guard it from prying eyes nobody is entirely certain. He vanishes almost as soon as he appears.

The churchyard at Hathersage is haunted by a very tall man indeed. This is said to be Little John, the famous companion of Robin Hood. His grave lies in the churchyard and its size indicates that the man buried there was around 8ft tall.

In 1326 a terrible storm hit Dunwich, Suffolk. The waves smashed the harbour and washed three churches and dozens of houses into the sea. On still nights the phantom sound of church bells from the lost churches will drift up from beneath the waves to echo across the beach.

A ghostly monk haunts a church in Bristol.

The fine church of St Bartholomew the Great lies just off Smithfield in London. This mighty Norman church was built in 1123 on the orders of Rahere, a courtier to King Henry I. Rahere had a vision one night in which Christ ordered him to found a monastery and become a monk. Rahere poured his worldly wealth into the foundation and took the holy vows to become its first abbot. The church he constructed was large enough to be a cathedral, and although the nave was demolished in the Reformation, it is still able to impress visitors with its sombre, dimly lit bulk. The phantom Rahere is seen most often standing as if deep in thought close to his tomb beside the high altar.

The ghost of eighteenth-century poet Alexander Pope walks his local parish church of St Mary's, Twickenham.

The church at Aston Clinton, Buckinghamshire, is haunted by a young woman carrying a crying baby. She is usually said to be an unmarried daughter of the local wealthy Lake family who fell pregnant and then died in childbirth. The family, it is said, hushed up the scandal but could never stop the ghost from walking.

York Minster is home to the ghost of a medieval mason. Those who admire one particular window in the West Front have found a figure suddenly standing beside them.

'I carved that,' at least one witness has heard the phantom declare before vanishing.

In 1642 Worcester Cathedral was occupied by the Parliamentarian army of the Duke of Essex. Armed guards were posted around the city which was known for its generally Royalist sympathies. One guard suddenly abandoned his post and ran into the cathedral before collapsing unconscious. His officers assumed he was drunk, but when the man came to he claimed to have been attacked by a ghostly bear. Odd as the story might appear, a phantom bear has been reported in the Cathedral Close off and on ever since.

MALEVOLENT PHANTOMS

The notorious 'Man in Black' frequents the area around the abbey and the adjacent Pump Room in the city of Bath. The Pump Room was built in 1789 to cater to the fashionable members of society who came to Bath to take the waters. The Man in Black wears a short cloak that billows around him in even the calmest weather, and has a tall black hat. These fashions would date him to the late 1600s, when Bath was a quiet county town with no sign of the elegant fashionable grandeur it would soon acquire. All those who have seen the Man in Black say that he has a scowl upon his face and exudes a feeling of malevolence.

A view of Bath Abbey. The pavements around the abbey are haunted by a man dressed in black who exudes an air of malevolence.

A series of nasty road accidents on the A256 at Cliffsend in Kent during the 1970s was blamed on the ghost of a murderer who was hanged on the gibbet that formerly stood on the site.

The ghost of a beautiful young lady named Silky haunts the bridge just south of Black Heddon in Northumberland. She is said to be the phantom of a local woman who lived in Black Heddon during the eighteenth century, and who was known as much for her spiteful nature as her good looks. Her ghost has been blamed for the high number of motor accidents that have taken place on and beside the bridge.

The massive castle at Skipton, Yorkshire, stands imposingly at the head of the broad High Street. The ghost here manifests itself only when the owner is about to die. At such times a coach pulled by four horses comes to a halt outside the main gates. A man dressed in black descends, strides up to the gates and knocks. Then the apparition vanishes.

A woman with a lantern walks the beach at St Ives, Cornwall, to herald a coming shipwreck in the area.

The retired army officer Major Thomas Weir amazed his Edinburgh neighbours in 1670 when he suddenly confessed to being a witch of awesome and deeply satanic power. The evidence he produced was overwhelming, so he was duly executed along with his sister in the Grassmarket. His ghost, accompanied by his magical black staff, stalks the area and brings bad luck to whoever sees him.

The ghost of Lady Margaret Pomeroy haunts Berry Pomeroy Castle in Devon. She was jilted by her fiancé and now seeks to lure men to dangerous parts of the ruin where they will suffer injury or death.

A sinister man in black haunts the churchyard in Ashwell, Hertfordshire, and is said to bring bad luck.

On 4 August 1577, a church service at Blythburgh was interrupted when the church door was thrown open and a gigantic black hound paced silently into the sacred building. With fire flashing from its eyes and sparks glittering along its teeth, the dark dog glared malevolently at the startled congregation. Then with a bound, the dog leapt up; the roof caved in as the spire came crashing down, causing injury and mayhem among the good folk of Blythburgh.

A church service in the town of Blythburgh was interrupted by a demonic black dog.

The Battle of Killiecrankie was fought in 1689 between rebels under John Graham, Viscount Dundee, who supported the exiled King James II and a government army under Hugh MacKay. Dundee was killed in the fighting, though his men avenged his death by winning a stunning victory. The battlefield is haunted by a young woman dressed in highland tartan who slips about furtively while carrying a wickedly long knife. She is said to exude a feeling of malevolence and evil.

HAPPY GHOSTS

Richard, Earl Howe, one of the great naval heroes of the eighteenth century, haunts his old house in Great Pulteney Street, Bath. Howe joined the navy at the age of thirteen and commanded his own ship at the early age of just twenty. He fought in the Mediterranean, the Atlantic and the Pacific, but his great moment came in 1793 when he led the Channel Fleet to a spectacular victory over the French in a battle that quickly became known as the 'Glorious First of June'. Wealthy, ennobled and famous, Howe then retired from the sea to his house in Bath. His ghost appears in a cocked hat and long cloak, beneath which can be glimpsed the glitter of gold braid and jewelled medals. He was happy here in Bath and appears in his finest outfit.

Avenbury Church in Herefordshire is haunted by a former organist, who comes back to play sacred tunes on his old instrument.

The cheerful phantom of Nell Gwynne – the mistress of King Charless II – has been seen in her old home of Salisbury Hall in Hertfordshire.

Corpus Christi College in Oxford is home to the sedate spectre of Dr Butts, the master of the college from 1626 to 1632. This blameless phantom potters about the upper storey of Old Court where he had his chambers.

The Grey Lady of Washington Old Hall in Tyne and Wear seems content to sit and relax in what was once the private parlour. She is seen several times each year sitting in an old upright wooden chair that is every bit as spectral as she is herself. The temperature of the room usually drops suddenly when she is about to appear.

The ghost haunting the George and Dragon at West Wycombe is that of Sukie, a serving girl who worked here in the late eighteenth century. She had an accidental fall and died in the pub before a doctor could reach her. Her graceful spectral form seems to prefer the early morning for her visits, and is usually seen in the kitchens or nearby corridors where she spent most of her life.

The eighteenth-century playwright Richard Sheridan haunts no. 11 Royal Crescent in Bath. It was from this house that he eloped with Elizabeth Linley on 18 March 1772. He is seen most often alone, but sometimes walking arm-in-arm with his love.

ANCIENT GHOSTS

Chester boasts a Roman soldier who paces endlessly between the ruined Roman tower beside Newgate in the city walls and the excavated ruins of the amphitheatre. According to local legend the phantom is that of a decurian of the XI Legion Adiutrix, stationed here in the first century. He fell in love with a local girl, but was betrayed. The girl's father heard that he would open a side gate to slip out to meet his love. One night the father and a band of warriors pounced, killed the decurian and slipped into the city to steal and plunder.

The cellar of the Treasurer's House in York is haunted by a whole column of Roman soldiers. These men come from the end of the Roman occupation, being fourth-century auxiliaries armed with oval shields and long spears. The column is led by a mounted officer and accompanied by a trumpeter. According to those who have seen them, the soldiers appear tired and dispirited.

Bindon Hill in Dorset is haunted by a troop of armoured men who march about, usually on nights of a spring tide. They are usually said to be Romans, but they are seen most often close to a Bronze Age burial barrow.

Several Bronze Age barrows lie on Dorset's Bottlebush Down, and they are haunted by what may be Britain's oldest ghost. The ghost is that of a horseman with bare legs and a long, loose coat. The rider waves a sword over his head in an aggressive fashion as he gallops over the downs. The ghost always vanishes beside the same low, round barrow. Presumably it is the ghost of the man buried within.

HAUNTED PUBS

The Wheatsheaf in Newport on the Isle of Wight is haunted by Anne Blundell. Her husband was an officer in an Irish regiment posted here in the Napoleonic Wars. He was shot in a duel, but took weeks to die as he lay in the pub, tended by his anguished wife. Anne moved back to her family and remarried a few years later, but her ghost returns here. Perhaps she never got over the death of her first husband?

The White Hart in Blythburgh, Suffolk, is haunted by a short, old man who is thought to be a monk.

The Brushmaker's Arms in Upham, Hampshire, is haunted by the ghost of the man who built the place before being murdered here. Mr Chickett built the pub as a brush factory and made a tidy fortune from the brushes he made. He would sit upstairs in his bedroom, counting out his gold and silver coins before stashing them away safely in a hidden compartment. Then, one morning his workers arrived to find old Mr Chickett battered to death, his room ransacked and his money stolen. Ever since then, the ghost has walked. It takes the unusual form of a mere outline of a man, like a shadow on the wall, that slides silently along the upstairs corridor.

The George at Hatherleigh, Devon, is haunted by the phantom of a pretty young woman – who appears stark naked on an upstairs corridor.

The Queen's Head at Winchelsea is haunted by a former landlord who died here in 1900. His body was laid out in the bar and a riotous wake followed the funeral.

The Saracen's Head in Southwell dates back to the 1180s, though the ghost is much less ancient, dating only to August 1642. In that month, King Charles I stayed here on his way to Nottingham where he raised the Royal Standard and so began the Civil War against parliament. In May 1646, King Charles was back – and this time he was a beaten man. The following day he was captured by his enemies and soon afterwards his life was ended on the executioner's block in London. The rooms the king occupied are still there, and it is in and near this suite that the king's ghost is to be encountered. He does not look much like a regal monarch, more like the dispirited and broken man that he was on his second visit. He wears travel-stained clothes of coarse wool and boots splashed with mud.

The Bull Inn at Henley is haunted by a young woman who is often accompanied by the scent of candles. The haunting is usually blamed on the fact that the old stables were used as a mortuary for a while in the early twentieth century.

The Feathers Hotel in Ludlow has two very different ghosts. The first is a young lady dressed in fashions that are unmistakably those of the 1960s – a very short mini skirt and a tight top. She is seen most often as she walks into the foyer from the street, and then vanishes. Up on the second floor is the phantom of a middle-aged man. This is usually identified as the spirit of the man who built the Feathers to be his home: Rees Jones. Jones was a successful lawyer who built the house in 1619 when he got married.

ROYAL GHOSTS

King William Rufus is said to haunt the spot in the New Forest where he was murdered in 1100. His ghost then walks off along the track toward Winchester, along which his body was carried for burial.

King George II haunts Kensington Palace. He died while awaiting news from his native Hanover, which had been delayed by contrary winds in the Channel. His ghost peers up at the wind vane muttering, 'Why don't they come? Why don't they come?'

Mary Queen of Scots was a long way from home when she was executed in Northamptonshire, and her ghost remains in this foreign spot.

Mary Queen of Scots is said to haunt the Talbot Hotel in Oundle, Northamptonshire. The sad monarch was executed at nearby Fotheringhay Castle. When the castle was demolished the grand oak staircase was brought to the Talbot Hotel – and the ghost seems to have come with it.

Anne Boleyn, the second of the ill-fated wives of King Henry VIII, haunts the Tower of London. Or at least she did. Nobody has reported seeing her stalking the scene of her execution for more than fifty years.

Anne Boleyn also haunts her childhood home of Hever Castle in Kent. She is said to walk over the bridge leading to the house and is seen more often in the winter than the summer.

Catherine Howard, the fifth wife of Henry VIII, followed Anne Boleyn to the scaffold. Her phantom may be met in the Long Gallery of Hampton Court Palace, and was recently caught on a security camera emerging from a doorway.

Bonnie Prince Charlie, the exiled Stuart prince who held himself to be the legitimate king as Charles III, haunts Derby Cathedral. Derby was the closest that he ever got to being king. Having led an army of Scottish highlanders down as far as the town, Charles was then forced to turn back by the gathering forces of the armies loyal to George II.

The Duke of Monmouth was an illegitimate son of King Charles II who claimed to be legitimate and so the rightful heir to the throne after the death of his father. He landed at Lyme Regis in front of cheering crowds, but support was slow to gather and he was defeated at the Battle of Sedgemoor and then executed by his vengeful uncle, James II. Monmouth's ghost rides up from the harbour at Lyme Regis heading inland. Those who have seen him say he waves cheerfully as if to invisible crowds seen only by him.

HAUNTED ROADS

The main road through Kingston St Mary, Somerset, is haunted by a horseman riding a grey mare. Local legend has it that the phantom is that of Squire Surtees who lived here in the eighteenth century.

The B3170 south of Taunton is haunted by a man on a prancing horse. Whether he is linked to the nearby racecourse or not, nobody seems to know.

The A512 at Thringstone in Leicestershire is haunted by a ghostly lady in a grey dress, said to be a nun from the nearby Grace Dieu Priory. In 1982 a bus driver stopped to pick her up, but she vanished abruptly instead of boarding the bus.

The old Portsmouth Road, Cobham, Surrey, crosses the River Mole just south of the village. The bridge is haunted by a ghostly man who is described as being astonishingly ugly – poor chap.

The A428 turns a sharp corner just outside Brandon, Warwickshire. The spot is haunted by a ghostly lorry which careers off the road at speed.

RELIGIOUS GHOSTS

A nun haunts the village of Hinton Martell in Dorset.

Archbishop Simon Sudbury of Canterbury was beheaded in 1380. His body was buried in Canterbury, but his head was interred at Sudbury in Suffolk. His ghost has been seen in the church at Sudbury, presumably searching for his head.

A group of about a dozen monks has been seen clustered around the Great Tower of the medieval abbey at Bury St Edmunds. A number of monks were killed during a riot here in 1327.

A phantom monk has been seen walking from Bruern Abbey to Tangley Hall in Oxfordshire.

The phantom of Miles Coverdale, Bishop of Exeter in the reign of Edward VI, has been seen standing beside his tomb in St Magnus the Martyr, close to London Bridge.

Monks chanting late medieval plainsong haunt the ruins of Beaulieu Abbey in Hampshire.

Michelham Priory in Sussex is haunted by a monk in a grey habit – but also by a pretty lady in a long, blue silk dress.

A monk haunts the transepts of Westminster Abbey in the days around Christmas. In 1934 a clairvoyant claimed that the ghost had declared its name to be Father Benedictus and that he had died in the 1530s.

A group of monks has been seen in the Priory Orchard at Kings Langley in Hertfordshire.

MILITARY GHOSTS

Wardour Castle in Wiltshire is haunted by the phantom of the Lady Arundel who held the fortress for the king against the Roundheads during the Civil War.

Admiral Thomas Hardy, who cradled the dying Admiral Nelson in his arms at the Battle of Trafalgar, haunts his old home in Victoria Walk, Cheltenham.

Thousands of phantom soldiers have been seen recreating the Battle of Edgehill, fought in Warwickshire in 1642.

In February 1643 the poet Sydney Godolphin led a troop of Royalist cavalry to Chagford in Devon. The Cavaliers were ambushed by Roundheads and Godolphin was cut down. He was carried to the Three Crowns, where he died. His ghost haunts the inn to this day.

A portrait of the ghostly cavalier who haunts the inn at Chagford, Devon.

The battlefield of Bosworth is a controversial one for historians with at least two sites near the village being claimed as the scene of the struggle. The ghostly knights are in no doubt, they are seen in woodland nearer to Sutton Cheney than Market Bosworth.

The phantom knights of Bosworth battlefield are a sad lot.

SAD SPECTRES

In the seventeenth century a young lady from Zeals House, Wiltshire, eloped with a good-looking servant with whom she was in love. She was never seen again, but very soon her ghost began to haunt the gardens. In the 1890s a female skeleton was found in nearby woods and is widely believed to have been that of the unfortunate young woman who was murdered by her lover for her jewels.

In the late nineteenth century the body of a woman, dressed in rich clothes, was washed up on the beach near Teignmouth. The body was buried in an unmarked grave in the churchyard. Her phantom haunts the stretch of beach where she was found. Walking disconsolately along the shoreline, the richly dressed lady in a long gown will pause occasionally to stare out to sea.

Lord Marney died in 1523 before he could finish building a new manor at Layer Marney, Essex. His son finished the house, but to different plans and Lord Marney returns in spectral form to protest at the changes.

At any time of the year a visitor to the Christ's College, Cambridge, may come cross a stooped figure shuffling quietly around the Fellows' Garden. This is the penitent ghost of a Fellow from two centuries ago named Christopher Rounds. He killed another Fellow of the college on this spot and, although he escaped the noose, his spirit returns still in the hope of achieving forgiveness.

The Silent Pool in Surrey is haunted by the phantom of a beautiful medieval maiden who drowned here. Witnesses differ as to whether she appears clothed or naked.

The ghost of Lydia Atley lurks by the lychgate in Ringstead in Northamptonshire. She was murdered by a local married farmer when she fell pregnant by him, but her body was never found. It is assumed that she is trying to lead people to her grave so that her body can be given a decent burial.

Deeply disconsolate are the shadows that lurk near the old burial ground at Princetown, high on Dartmoor. Locally it is said that these are the phantoms of the dozens of French prisoners of war who died in captivity here during the Napoleonic Wars. Far from home and no doubt miserable in captivity, they lie buried in unmarked graves. No wonder spirits wander here.

The town hall at Woodbridge is haunted by a man dressed in eighteenth-century clothing and bearing a mournful face.

4

SEA SERPENTS & LAKE MONSTERS

Over the centuries there have been persistent reports of large animals living in the sea that do not resemble any known animal. They are not whales or turtles, seals or fish, but they are large – sometimes enormous. These creatures have been sighted many times, often at close quarters and in some detail, but they are not accepted by mainstream science. A key problem with the large creatures seen at sea is that no solid evidence has been produced to prove that they exist. No bodies, nor parts of bodies, have ever been brought back nor has anybody ever claimed to have caught a live example. There has also been an element of folklore and snobbery about the subject. Tales told by sailors have long been considered unreliable by respectable landsmen, and sometimes with reason. In the past, sailors have delighted in exaggerating the truth in order to mislead those who have not travelled as widely as themselves. As a result any report coming from a sailor was discounted by mainstream scientists.

That this attitude was wrong has been proved by the story of the 'rogue wave'. Seamen had long reported that on very rare occasions they ran into monstrous waves that were far larger and more powerful than any others. In the most extreme storms, waves regularly reach about 32ft in height, and sometimes around 42ft. The rogue waves, however, were reported to be up to 115ft tall and to be of a quite different form: they had a near-vertical front unlike the slopes of normal waves. Some of these waves were reported by highly qualified and respected officers, and yet scientists refused to believe the stories. Then, in 1995, scientific instruments on the Draupner oil platform in the North Sea measured a wave some 85ft tall. At last scientists began taking the old stories seriously and began investigating this rare phenomenon.

The current evidence for the existence of at least one species of large, unrecognised sea animal is in many ways stronger than the evidence for the rogue wave was before 1995. There are numerous eyewitness reports and clear, detailed descriptions. Many of the reports match each other, which would seem to indicate that the witnesses are seeing the same thing rather than inventing imaginary monsters to create an exciting story. Some researchers believe that there are between two and six types of large sea animal as yet unrecognised by science.

In recent years the number of sightings of gigantic sea creatures has fallen. Ocean-going ships are today very different from in the past. Modern ships have smaller crews, better crew accommodation and are more reliable than those in the past. The smaller crews and installation of televisions and computers mean that there are fewer men on board who, in off-duty moments, have little better to do than stare out to sea. The reliability of modern ships means that they tend to stay in the well-travelled sea lanes. Unlike sailing ships of old, they are less likely to find themselves in obscure areas of ocean.

Quite the opposite is true of lake monster sightings, which have increased dramatically in the past fifty years or so. Before 1950 very few large animals were reported as being seen in freshwater lakes, but after that date the number of sightings has risen steadily. In part this is due to the fact that more people are spending time beside or on lakes than ever before. With more leisure time and more money to spend on holidays, increasing numbers of people are spending time boating on lakes, sunbathing on their shores or simply travelling beside them. And the building of more and more roads to remoter regions means that a great many lakes that previously had few human visitors are now familiar to thousands.

In terms of credibility, the reports of large sea creatures have a clear advantage. There are vast areas of ocean in which an animal may live without being detected. If the creature does not need to surface to breathe air, it could remain submerged throughout its entire life. Moreover, there are undeniably huge stocks of food in the ocean on which a population of large animals could feed. Lakes, on the other hand, are much smaller than the oceans. This not only makes it much less likely that a large creature could live within a lake undetected, but also means that they contain much less food on which such animals could live.

EARLY REPORTS

In 1734 a Christian missionary team headed by Hans Egede saw a 'very terrible sea monster' off the coast of Greenland. Egede wrote, 'It had a long, sharp snout and blew like a whale,

The sea serpent reported by Hans Egede in 1734. The illustration was drawn with the assistance of a member of Egede's crew.

had broad, large flappers and the body was covered with a hard skin and was very wrinkled.' The creature raised its head about 30ft out of the water and was about 90ft long. The body was described as being similar to that of a snake. In 1741 one of Egede's team drew a picture of the monster. The drawing by Bing was included in a map published by Povel Egede, the son of Hans, who was producing a book about his father's work.

In 1746 Lorenz von Ferry, the chief pilot at Bergen in Norway sighted a 'sea snake' off Molde.

'The head was held 2ft above the surface of the water and resembled that of a horse. It was a greyish colour and the mouth was black and very large. It had large black eyes and a long pale mane. Beside the head we saw seven folds or coils of this snake with a fathom (6ft) between each fold.' Von Ferry fired a shotgun at the creature, which then dived out of sight. Worried that nobody would believe him, von Ferry got two of the sailors rowing his boat to appear in front of a magistrate to swear their descriptions of the creature.

In 1746 Lorenz von Ferry, the chief pilot at Bergen in Norway, took a shot at a sea serpent, but did not seem to do it any real injury.

THE GLOUCESTER SEA SERPENT

In the summer of 1817 a mysterious creature appeared several times in Massachusetts Bay, near Gloucester. It stayed for several weeks and was seen by dozens of people. A Boston society of gentlemen interested in wildlife interviewed many of the witnesses and produced a report on the creature.

Fisherman Amos Story was the first to see the creature, on 10 August. He stated, 'His head appeared shaped much like the head of a sea turtle, and he carried his head 12in above the surface of the water. His head was larger than the head of any dog that I ever saw. He moved very rapidly, I should say a mile in three minutes. I saw about 10ft of his body.'

A merchant ship master, Solomon Allen, saw the animal on 13 August.

'I should judge him to be between 80 and 90ft in length and about the size of a half-barrel, apparently having joints from his head to his tail. His head formed something like that of a rattle snake, but nearly as large as the head of a horse. When

A woodcut of the Gloucester sea serpent of 1817, drawn from a sketch by an eyewitness.

he disappeared, he sunk directly down and would next appear at 200yds from where he disappeared in two minutes. His colour was a dark brown.'

Also on 13 August, ship's carpenter Matthew Gaffney was in a small boat when the animal surfaced just 30ft away.

'He was coming at us, but he sunk down and went directly under our boat and made his appearance at about 100yds from where he sunk. He did not turn down like a fish, but appeared to settle directly down like a rock.'

Five days later William Pearson saw the creature off Cape Ann.

'I should say that he was nothing short of 70ft in length. The top of his head appeared flat and was raised 8in above the surface of the water. He passed by my boat at about 30yds distance. His colour was dark brown.'

On 28 August the crew of the schooner *Laura* saw the creature further out to sea. It was moving fast.

'About 6in in height his body and head were out of water, and as I should judge about 15ft in length. He had a head like a snake, rather larger than his body and blunt. He threw out his tongue about 2ft in length, the end of it appeared to me to resemble a harpoon. He moved at about 14 miles per hour. He was of a dark chocolate colour and I should suppose the neck was 2½ft in diameter. His motion was very steady, a little up and down.'

SEA SERPENTS

On 24 July 1891 Mr A. Matthews was in a boat off East Cape, New Zealand, when he saw a gigantic snake-like animal. The creature was about 60ft long, had a black back and white belly and had a pair of paddles near its head. The creature raised its head vertically up out of the water, then turned slowly around before diving out of sight.

On 1 August 1891 A. Kerr, the chief officer, and other crew members of the SS *Rotomahana* spotted what may have been the same creature seen by Matthews. The serpent was reported as being 70ft long and about 4ft wide. It had flippers near its head.

On 15 May 1833 five army officers based at Halifax, Nova Scotia, went out in a yacht for a leisure trip. They sighted a gigantic snake-like creature about 80ft long. They wrote an account of the creature stating, 'The head of the creature we set down at about 6ft in length, and the height of the neck at about the same. The neck in thickness equalled the bole of a moderate-sized tree. The head and neck [were] of a dark brown colour streaked with white in irregular streaks.'

In August 1845 geologist J. Dawson of Nova Scotia came across a snake-like creature about 100ft long splashing about the shallows off Merigomish. It was very dark grey or black in colour and had a head similar to that of a seal. Dawson watched the beast for about 30 minutes, after which it swam off out to sea.

In October 1844 a serpent swam past the pier at Arisaig, Nova Scotia. It moved with long undulations of its body. The body was estimated to be 60ft long and 3ft thick. The head was rounded and blunt at the snout.

On 15 April 1856 the merchant ship *Imogen* was south of the Azores when 'an immense snake' came into view. It was about 40ft long and had a head like that of a snake. When it was about 700yds from the ship, the creature slowed and lifted its head as if to look at the ship, then it changed direction and swam off north at speed.

On 21 August 1872 the yacht *Leda* was off the Isle of Skye when the six passengers saw a long creature that writhed through the sea in a series of undulations. After the beast had been in view for 20 minutes it seemed to sight the yacht and began swimming toward it at speed, throwing up spray as it did so. When it was about 100yds from the yacht the creature dived, swam under the yacht and then resurfaced half a mile away. The creature was black or very dark brown and had fins behind the head.

The Sea Orm (Norwegian for serpent) as illustrated in a book by Olaus Magnus in 1555. The description was based on a number of reports.

On 28 July 1845 four local men were out fishing on Romsdalsfjord, Norway. They sighted a serpent-like creature that had a pair of fins on the forward part of its body. The head was held vertically clear of the water on a neck about 7ft long and had a pointed snout. About 40ft of the body could be seen above the water, but there seemed to be more submerged behind it.

BROAD-BODIED CREATURES

In 1820 the merchant ship *Lady Combermere* came across what the lookout took to be an upturned ship's hull wallowing in the waves of the Bay of Biscay. The master, George Sandford, steered for the object and later wrote a description of what he saw.

'I saw a hump at one extreme resembling the point of a triangular rock. This tapered to a distance I certainly believe 70 or 100ft, and the water broke over it. I was undetermined in mind what it could be or whether I should tack the ship. It all at once disappeared and, to my great astonishment, a head and neck resembling something of a snake's made its appearance, erected about 6ft above the water. It all at once vanished.'

On 2 June 1877 the royal yacht *Osborne* was off Sicily when Commander Hugh Pearson and his men sighted a creature. It was seen from behind as it surfaced and swam away. In form it seemed to be a gigantic turtle. The head was about 6ft wide, the body about 20ft across and the two flippers visible on either side about 15ft long. It was estimated to be about 50ft long, though given the angle from which it was seen this may not be accurate.

In June 1890 Miss S. Lovell was living on Great Sandy Island off the Queensland coast. One morning she saw a giant turtle-like creature moving about in the shallows near the beach. It was about 30ft long. The domed body had a fish tail behind and a heavy neck and head in front. She watched it for about half an hour before it swam out to sea. The local aborigines told Miss Lovell that they beast was called a 'moha-moha' and that it sometimes came ashore, when they would kill it and eat it.

In 1905 the yacht *Valhalla* was off Parahiba in Brazil when the two men aboard, E.G. Meade-Waldo and M. Nicholl, spotted a large turtle-like creature. The head was held clear of the water on a neck about 10ft long, while the large body was mostly beneath the water. A fin was sometimes visible rising from the creature's back. The upper surfaces of the animal were dark brown while the undersides had a silvery appearance.

In 1920 Thomas Muir was an officer on the SS *Tyne* steaming from Casablanca to Brazil. In the mid-Atlantic, Muir and the crew sighted what they thought was derelict wreckage with an upright mast. The ship steered to investigate, at which the object began to move. Muir studied it through binoculars and saw a head on a tall neck, with a rounded body in the sea beneath. He estimated the neck to be about 30ft tall and the body to have been about 60ft long.

In August 1923 HMS *Kellett* was in the North Sea off the Thames Estuary when a crew member drew Captain Haselfoot's attention to what seemed to be the head and neck of a creature about 200yds away. The head was held on a vertical neck about 7ft tall. The object sank vertically down, then surfaced again for five seconds before sinking again.

On 22 May 1964 the fishing boat *Friendship* out of New Bedford, Massachusetts, came across a creature that was about 30ft long and had a small head perched on top of a thin neck. The creature was swimming slowly and remained in sight for 20 minutes.

CRUISING CREATURES

In 1829 the merchant ship *Royal Saxon* was passed by an animal swimming fast in the opposite direction. It was seen by passenger R. Davidson, Captain Petrie and two crew members. The creature was low in the water showing its head and about 30ft of length above the surface, but with an estimated 60ft more below the surface. It moved in a straight line without apparently undulating its body, leading Davidson to suggest that it had flippers out of sight. As it passed, the creature turned its head to look at the ship.

On 6 August 1848 the captain and crew of HMS *Daedalus* sighted a curious animal at close quarters in the South Atlantic.

HMS Daedalus *shown here with the mysterious creature seen by her crew in the foreground.*

Captain M'Quhae wrote a detailed report and produced sketches of the animal. The animal had a rounded head held just clear of the sea on a neck. The neck extended back in a straight line and about 60ft was visible, though M'Quhae thought that there was more under the water. Although the creature was moving at about 12 miles per hour, it did not wriggle or undulate, so the means of propulsion must have been hidden under the surface. The head looked like that of a snake and the neck was about 16in thick. There was what looked like a mane or a bunch of seaweed just behind the head. M'Quhae was a highly experienced officer who had been decorated by King William IV. His detailed notes and drawings forced scientists to take notice of the possibility of a large, unknown sea animal. When no further proof appeared the scientists quietly dismissed the incident.

In 1849 the crew of HMS *Plumper* sighted an unusual creature in the Bay of Biscay. It was moving at about 2 miles per hour.

The head was raised out of the water and came to a point and about 20ft of the body was visible.

On 4 December 1893 the SS *Umfuli* was steaming off the Cape of Good Hope when Captain R. Cringle sighted a large animal swimming in the opposite direction. He called the passengers on deck to see it. The creature was about 75ft long and held a small head clear of the water on a neck about 15ft long. It was moving fast, throwing up spray as it swam. Cringle steered toward it, then followed it for about half an hour so that everyone got a good look. The creature was still swimming strongly when the *Umfuli* turned back on its course and steamed away.

CROCODILE MONSTERS

In 1838 HMS *Fly* was cruising off California when it encountered a large, crocodile-like creature. It was reported as having the head of an alligator, but with a much longer neck. Instead of legs it had four flippers similar to those of a turtle.

CANADIAN LAKES

The most famous lake monster in Canada is 'Ogopogo', said to live in Lake Okanagan in British Columbia. The lake covers 135 square miles and has a depth of about 650ft. Ogopogo has been seen from the late nineteenth century. Descriptions vary with some witnesses reporting a snake-like animal and others describing a creature with a bulky body, flippers and a long neck.
   A traditional rhyme goes:

> I'm looking for the Ogopogo.
> The funny little Ogopogo.
> It's mother was a shrimp and its father was a whale
> and I want to put a little bit of sugar on its tail.

Lake Manitoba is said to be home to a snake-like creature about 30ft long. It has been seen several times since 1906, but there is no detailed description available.

Turtle Lake in Saskatchewan is said to be home to a man-eating fish of gigantic proportions. No modern sightings have been reported, so it may be an old tribal legend.

Lake Winnipegosis covers 2,072 square miles in Manitoba. It is said to be home to a creature nicknamed 'Winnipogo'. The beast is said to be a dark brown serpent about 25ft long that eats fish. One witness said that Winnipogo had a horn on the back of its head.

Crescent Lake in Newfoundland is reportedly home to a gigantic eel. Witnesses have estimated its length as being over 30ft. It has been known to attack human scuba divers.

'Igopogo' is a seal-like animal said to live in Lake Simcoe, Ontario. It has a head shaped like that of a dog, but enormous in size. One witness said that it came out on shore to bask in the sun.

Muskrat Lake in Ontario is reputedly home to 'Mussie', a creature that is routinely described as being like a walrus. In the 1990s Mussie was used as the centrepiece of a marketing campaign to publicise the area as a tourist resort. A prize of $1 million was put up for the capture of a live Mussie, but no creature was captured.

In 1934 a rotund creature was reported to be surfacing in Lake Ontario, near Kingston. The 'monster' was soon revealed to be an old wooden barrel painted to look monstrous.

Ontario's Lake Temiskaming is said to hide a gigantic fish, dubbed the 'Mugwump' locally. It may be a giant sturgeon, a fish that can grow to be 20ft long.

Lake Memphremagog straddles the border between the US and Canada. Witnesses have reported seeing a reptilian creature that looks like a whale about 40ft long. The beast is known as 'Memphre' in the local press.

Quebec's Lake Pohenegamook is said to have a resident monster dubbed 'Ponik' by locals, but details are scarce.

MONSTERS IN AMERICA

In 1915 sightings of a strange animal in the White River of Arkansas began to be made. The creature was said to be 20ft long and 5ft wide, shaped a bit like a seal and to have a horn on its head. It made a noise described as being a blend of a cow's moo and horse's neigh. The monster is now considered to have been an elephant seal from the Gulf of Mexico that got lost and swam up the Mississippi to the White River.

Lake Elsinore in southern California is rumoured to have a monster, but details are scarce. It was dubbed 'Hamlet' by the local press after the fictional Danish prince who lived in Elsinore Castle.

Named 'Tessie' in imitation of the Nessie in Loch Ness, the creature said to live in California's Lake Tahoe is reported to be a snake-like animal about 60ft long.

Elizabeth Lake in California was known during colonial times as La Laguna de Diablo, or Devil's Lake, due to a local tribal legend that stated that a hideous monster lived in it waters.

Idaho's Payette Lake has long been rumoured to be home to a large animals of some kind. The creature has been dubbed 'Sharlie' and is said to resemble a crocodile about 35ft long, but with flippers in place of legs.

Lake Erie is said to be home to 'Bessie', a name chosen to liken it to Nessie of Loch Ness. It is said to be about 40ft long and to resemble a python.

The monster of Lake Thunderbird in Oklahoma is unique in that it is said to be a freshwater octopus of prodigious size. The lake was created in 1961 by the damming of the Little River.

A large walrus-like creature is said to live in Bear Lake, Utah, but some investigators believe it is a hoax of some kind.

Between 1840 and 1880 reports were made of a strange animal in the Great Salt Lake of Utah. It was reportedly shaped like a crocodile, but having the head of a horse.

Spanning Vermont and Quebec, Lake Champlain is said to be home to a monster named 'Champ' by locals. The monster is said to have a rotund body, stumpy tail and elongated neck. It apparently swims by means of four flippers. Reports began to be made in the late nineteenth century and have continued to the present day. The monster is used to promote tourism in the area and many local businesses feature the creature in their logos and promotional material.

LOCH NESS

Easily the most famous lake monster in the world is Nessie, a beast that is said to inhabit Loch Ness. Despite its great fame, however, the evidence for Nessie is relatively slight. There are a few sightings from the nineteenth century or earlier, but the number of reports increased only after a road was built along the loch shore in 1932 linking Inverness with Fort Augustus. The road made it possible for passers by to view the loch clearly for the first time – before 1932 only the few local people spent much time by the loch. It is noteworthy that early reports often speak of Nessie coming out of the water, but later reports have the creature only in the loch.

In 1880 eight-year-old E. Bright was walking along the shore near Drumnadrochit with a friend. They saw a creature about the size of a small elephant waddle out of some woods on stump-like legs and waddle down to the loch. It had no tail to speak of, but had a long neck on top of which was perched a small head shaped like that of a snake. It splashed into the water and dived from sight. The boys later brought the elder Mr Bright to the spot and they found a series of three-toed footprints.

In 1875 a family, who preferred to remain anonymous, drove out of Inverness for a picnic beside the northern end of Loch Ness. They stopped near Tor Point and unpacked their meal. The family saw a creature that they described as being bigger than a rhinoceros, but with a long neck and long tail. It came lumbering across the grass toward them as if attracted by the food, then turned aside and splashed into the water where it dived beneath the surface.

In May 1933 the Loch Ness Water Bailiff, Alex Campbell, wrote an article for the *Inverness Courier* newspaper in which he collected together a number of reports – some of them anonymous – about a 'monster' living in the loch. Campbell claimed to have seen the creature himself. The article sparked off a lively debate in the letters column and is generally thought to have encouraged witnesses to come forward with tales that they had previously kept private for fear of ridicule.

On 5 June 1933, a young woman named Margaret Munro was walking to work when she spotted the beast on shore, close to the loch. She said it had a rotund body, long neck and small head and was dark grey in colour. It moved itself about on two short flippers or short legs at the front of its body. She said that she watched it for about 20 minutes at a range of about 150yds before it took to the water and dived from sight.

On 22 July 1933 London businessman George Spicer was driving along the south shore between Dores and Foyers when a large object crashed out of the woods on to the road ahead of him. Spicer said the animal was about 25ft long, had a body that was rounded and dark grey in colour. The head was on the end of a long neck and there was a tail. The creature waddled over the road, through some bracken and into the loch. It left behind a large area of flattened and crushed undergrowth.

In August 1933 Arthur Grant was motorcycling at night when he almost ran straight into a large object blocking the new road near Abriachan. He swerved and fell off his bike. Getting up, Grant saw a large, barrel-shaped object lumbering off the road toward the loch. He claimed to see a long neck and small head. With a splash the monster vanished.

In 1934 London surgeon Robert Wilson sent a photo to the *Daily Mail* newspaper that he claimed showed the head and neck of the Loch Ness monster. The photo became known as the Surgeon's Photograph and was widely reproduced. Analysis of the photo with modern techniques in the 1980s showed that the object was only 2ft tall, much smaller than Wilson had claimed. In 1994 sculptor Christian Spurling confessed that he had faked the photo using a wooden model. The motive was to gain revenge on the newspaper which had printed unfavourable articles about his father-in-law, Marmaduke Wetherell.

In 1943 C.B. Farrel was on duty watching the skies for German bombers when he saw the monster in the loch. He reported that it was about 30ft long and had a small head perched on top of a 5ft tall neck.

In December 1954 the crew of the fishing boat *Rival III* were alarmed to see on their sonar that a large object was following them at a depth of about 480ft. The object kept pace with the boat for about half a mile, then turned aside.

In 1960 an engineer named Tim Dinsdale stopped to look at the view, and saw a large object moving across the loch. He filmed it as it moved away from him, leaving behind it a strong wake. The film was shot in fairly poor light conditions and some suggested that the object was a man in a small boat. In 1993 the movie was subjected to computer enhancement. This showed that the object above the water was part of something much larger underneath the surface, which would have ruled out the object being a boat.

On 21 July 1961 Helen Stitt and her father were camping beside Loch Ness on a fishing trip. In the early evening they saw a sudden splashing from which arose a humped, rounded object. The object then swam off toward the centre of the loch where it slowly sank from view.

In 1972 a team led by Robert Rines placed underwater cameras and sonar equipment at various places in Loch Ness. They captured several images that appeared to show a creature similar to a prehistoric plesiosaur marine reptile. The most famous photo was dubbed the 'Flipper Photo' as it seemed to show a rhomboid flipper.

In 2003 the BBC paid for a detailed and exhaustive sonar search of Loch Ness. The search took several days, but ended having found nothing larger than a salmon. The sonar team concluded that the Loch Ness Monster did not exist.

OTHER SCOTTISH LOCHS

Loch Oich is said to be home to 'Wee Oichy'. This beast is reportedly 10ft long, had a small head shaped like that of a dog, long neck and humped back. Reports of the monster date back to the 1880s and in 1910 a young boy drowned after saying he had seen the beast. In 1961 a group of students launched a radio-controlled hoax monster that sparked a rash of sighting reports in the local press.

The tidal Loch Linnhe is said to be home to a humped creature about 30ft long. It has been seen rolling and splashing about on the surface.

Loch Quoich is reputedly home to a creature that is said to be carnivorous and to prey on sheep that come to drink from the lake waters.

The creature in Loch Arkaig is said to be dangerous to humans, though only if they antagonise it. The creature with a head similar to that of a horse was reported by the Earl of Malmesbury when on a shooting trip to the Highlands in 1857.

SCANDINAVIAN LAKES

'Gryttie' is the name given the animal said to lurk in Lake Gryttjen in Sweden. Sightings go back to the nineteenth century and seem to describe a form of vegetarian seal, perhaps akin to a manatee.

Lake Storsjön in Sweden is said to be home to a reptilian, snake-like beast about 19ft long with a head shaped like that of a dog. A row of spikes or spines is said to run down its back. The animal has been named 'Storsjöodjuret', which translates as 'the animal in Storsjön that is not really an animal'.

Norway's Lake Seljord is said to be home to a giant eel. Sightings date back to the eighteenth century and the creature has been named 'Selma'.

Varberg has an unusual creature that may be a seal. The 'lake' in question is really the moat around Varberg Castle. Something nearly 10ft long has been seen eating fish.

DOWN UNDER

Lake Coleridge in New Zealand covers 18 square miles and has a depth of about 650ft. During the 1970s and 1980s several locals reported sighting a large animal in the lake. It was described as being like a seal, but with four flippers. A local shepherd said it had attacked a lamb that was drinking from the lake. The creature was nicknamed 'Lakey', but it has not been seen since 1990.

Lake Argyle is an artificial lake in Western Australia covering 270 square miles and formed in 1971 by a dam across the Ord River. The monster, nicknamed 'Aggie', is said to be over 30ft long.

In the 1850s the first European settlers to arrive at Lake Modewarre in Victoria reported that the lake was home to a very large animal covered in feathers that sometimes came out on to land.

CHINESE LAKES

Lake Tian Chi fills a volcanic crater close to the border with North Korea. It covers about 4 square miles and is nearly 700ft deep. Since 1903 there have been sightings of a water creature rather larger than a cow. The animal is said to be shaped something rather like a giant seal, but to have a long neck at least 5ft long. In 2007, a Chinese television reporter named Zhuo Yongsheng visited the lake and shot a 20 minute video that he said showed a number of large animals in the lake. He also took some photos that seemed to show six animals swimming in pairs. In 2008 the American urban-folk band Mountain Goats released a song about the Tian Chi monster.

Lake Kanasi lies in the mountains of the far north-west of China. It covers about 17 square miles and is 600ft deep. Large animals have been sighted in it, but no clear description is available.

RUSSIAN MONSTERS

In July 1953 geologist V.A. Tverdokhlebov was working on the Sordongnokh Plateau of Siberia. One day he and an assistant, Boris Bashkatov, were studying rocks beside Lake Vorota when they heard a noise. Looking round they saw a creature swimming toward them. It was about 30ft long with a body about 12ft wide that bobbed up and down as it swam. The head was about 6½ft long and carried out of the water on a neck. The eyes were on the sides of the head, together with pale patches of skin. The rest of the animal was dark grey in colour. After approaching to within 100yds of the shore the creature dived out of sight. Tverdokhlebov spoke to local tribesmen who told him that they knew all about the animal in Lake Vorota. They said it would drag ducks from the surface and once grabbed a dog. One fisherman said that it had once approached his boat with its mouth agape as if about to attack, but had then swum off.

In 1963 a second scientific expedition reached Lake Vorota. They reported hearing stories of a large lake animal, but the only sighting was of a large, rounded object at a distance of over half a mile.

A third sighting of the Lake Vorota monster came in 1964 when an Estonian geologist sighted three humps emerging from the lake water just 100yds off shore. He grabbed a camera from his bag, but the humps had gone by the time he could focus on them.

In 1964 Moscow University sent a scientific expedition to study the tundra near Laptev in northern Siberia. Biologist N.F. Gladkikh was collecting animal samples along the shores of Lake Khaiyr when he walked around a group of trees and saw a large animal grazing grass. It was about 20ft long, had a large, rounded body supported on stubby feet or flippers and a small head perched on the end of a long neck. He ran to get his colleagues, but the animal had gone when they returned.

THE IRISH LOUGHS

On 18 May 1960 three Irish clergymen went fishing in a rowing boat on Lough Ree on the River Shannon. They saw a snake-like animal swimming with its head and neck raised some 18in out of the water. The creature was about 12ft long and, at its broadest, about 18in wide. The creature was in sight for about 3 minutes, then sank from sight.

Patrick Hanley was fishing on Lough Ree when his line was grabbed by something much stronger than any fish. The line was dragged from the reel then the boat began to be pulled toward the centre of the lake. Hanley cut the line.

Another fisherman, F.J. Waters, had his line seized by something that stirred up a great commotion on the water surface. The line was pulled very strongly straight down for about 70ft before the line snapped.

Lough Mask in County Mayo is said to be home to a crocodile-like creature about 12ft long.

Glendalough on County Wicklow has two lakes, the upper of which is supposed to be the haunt of a serpent.

Tipperary's Lough Nacorra is said to be home to a family of giant seals, each about the size of a small house.

A creature looking like a giant turtle about 12ft across has been seen in Lough Bray among the Wicklow Mountains. It is said to be dark grey in colour and to have the head and neck of a swan.

5

PREDICTIONS & CURSES

Both predictions and curses lay claim to the ability to peer into the future, and both are very often produced by the same people. The key difference is that while a person making a prediction claims to be able to see what will happen in the future, a person making a curse claims to be able to influence what will happen as well as being able to foresee it.

Traditionally both predictions and curses have been produced by those skilled in the occult arts. These folk have gone by many names in different cultures: witches, warlocks, shamans, priests and cunning men are but a few of the names used. Sometimes an entire but alien culture has been credited with the ability to make predictions and curses. Gypsies have recently been credited with these skills in Europe, while in earlier centuries the Saracens were believed to have such power.

These predictions have often been made after religious ceremonies or magical rituals have been completed. Many pagan deities were claimed to confer the ability to prophesy the future on to their priests or devotees. The Oracle at Delphi, sacred to the ancient Greek god Apollo, was only the most famous of the old pagan cults that claimed the ability to predict the future.

More recently the skills of prediction have come to be thought of as being more widespread. Many people have claimed that they have experienced glimpses of future events. Most such events come only once or twice in a lifetime, and they are frequently encountered as dreams. Some individuals, however, claim the ability to predict the future frequently and often. Such paranormal insights may come randomly and unbidden, or they may come only when the recipient has prepared themselves in some way and is actively seeking a glimpse into the future.

In recent years, curses have become less popular and less feared than they once were. Undoubtedly this is because the numbers of people willing to believe in them has declined, and those few who do still fear them do so with less intensity. However, there has been a growth in what might be termed jinxes. These are curses that have been incurred by accident rather than by design. While a curse is usually thought to have been inflicted by a person strong in paranormal powers, such as a witch or shaman, a jinx is incurred by the accidental breaking of a taboo or by inadvertently taking some action that is then regarded with hostility by some malevolent entity.

The people of the twenty-first century may believe less in witches, pagan gods and the like, but the efficacy of predictions, curses and jinxes remains undiminished. What has changed is that rather than simply accepting such events as being a perfectly normal part of the impact that the paranormal has on the human world, people are seeking scientific explanations. Elaborate studies have been carried out to try to test if precognition – the ability to know something before it happens – is a genuine phenomenon or merely a matter of random chance. The results are, to date, somewhat ambivalent. There are tantalising indications that some predictions do come true at a rate higher than would be expected by pure chance. But they do not do so with such regularity and reliability that the doubters have been silenced.

GREEK ORACLES

Located high on a mountainside in central Greece, the sacred enclosure of Delphi housed a temple dedicated to Apollo.

Inside the temple was a small room containing a three-legged stool positioned over a fissure in the rock. During the summer months the high priestess, called the Pythia, sat on this stool to commune with Apollo in a trance. The purpose of this was to answer questions posed by visiting dignitaries, many of whom asked about the future. Modern scientists believe that the volcanic fissure emitted ethylene gas, which would have induced a trance and rambling speech. The Pythia was famed for issuing advice that was always true, but often couched in obscure terms. Carved over the entrance to the Temple of Apollo at Delphi was possibly the best advice of all, 'Know yourself'.

In 650 BC Sparta was losing a war against Messenia and asked the Delphic Oracle for advice. The Pythia told the Spartans to ask their traditional enemy Athens to send them a commander for their army. The Athenians did not dare refuse an instruction from Apollo, but they did not want to help Sparta. They sent the Spartans a lame schoolmaster named Tyrtaeus to command

Apollo as sun god.

their armies. In the event, Tyrtaeus wrote a series of marching songs, battle cries and other poetic works that inspired the Spartan soldiers to victory.

In 594 BC Solon of Athens was granted dictatorial powers after winning a war against Salamis. The Pythia advised him, 'Seat yourself now amidships, for you are the pilot of Athens. Grasp the helm fast in your hands; you have many allies in your city.' Solon interpreted this to mean that he was popular enough to rely on votes, not the spears of his soldiers. He founded a democratic constitution that has inspired constitutions to the present day.

In 547 BC King Croesus of Lydia asked the Delphic Oracle for advice about an ongoing dispute with the Persian Empire. The Pythia replied, 'If Croesus made war on the Persians, he would destroy a mighty state.' Confident of victory, Croesus attacked the Persians. He was defeated and killed, and Lydia incorporated into the Persian Empire. Only then was it clear that the Pythia had foretold the destruction of Lydia, not of Persia.

In 491 BC the Spartans asked the Delphic Oracle if their king Demaratus was legitimate or not. Demaratus had been born eight months after his parents were married and there was concern that he was the son of his mother's first husband. The Pythia announced that Demaratus was no true king of Sparta, and so he was deposed. It was later revealed that the Pythia had been bribed by a Spartan nobleman to give the answer she did. The scandal was immense with the Pythia, the Spartan nobleman and others being imprisoned or exiled.

In 480 BC the Athenians sent an embassy to Delphi when threatened by a Persian invasion. The Pythia began by predicting that Athens would be burned to the ground, its temples filled with blood and stone towers tumbled down. But then the Pythia advised the Athenians that, 'your wooden wall shall not fall, but help you and your children,' even though the city of Athens was protected by stone walls. Only later did the Athenians realise that the Pythia meant that they should use their navy, their ships being made of wood, against the Persians.

The citizens of Delphi asked the Oracle for advice as an invading Persian army advanced in 480 BC. The Pythia announced, 'Pray to the winds, for they are the friends of the Greeks.' A few weeks later a mighty storm wrecked many of the Persian supply ships, starving the Persian army of food and hastening its retreat.

In 359 BC King Phillip II of Macedon was told by the Pythia, 'With silver spears you may conquer the world.' He then used the profits of the silver mines of Macedon to pay the wages of a hugely increased army and then made himself master of Greece.

In AD 67 the Roman Emperor Nero asked the Delphic Oracle how long he would live and was told, 'The number 73 marks the hour of your downfall.' Nero thought this meant that he would live to be seventy-three years old, but in fact he was overthrown in a revolt led by a general named Galba – who was seventy-three years old.

In AD 393 the Pythia announced, 'No shelter has Apollo, nor sacred laurel leaves; the fountains are now silent; the voice is stilled. It is finished.' A few weeks later the Emperor Theodosius ordered that all pagan temples, including Delphi, be closed down and that Christianity should be the only religion allowed in the Roman Empire.

At Dodona in north-western Greece was an oracle sacred to Zeus. The priests listened to the wind rustling in the leaves of the sacred oak trees to receive answers from the great god. If the priests ever washed their feet, however, they lost the power to interpret the sacred rustlings.

ANCIENT SEERS AND SIBYLS

Unlike the Oracle at Delphi which passed on messages from the gods, ancient seers said that they could see into the future.

The seer Megistias inspected the entrails of sacrificial animals to predict the future. At the Battle of Thermopylae in 480 BC he sacrificed a goat each morning for King Leonidas of Sparta. On the first two mornings Megistias fortold victory, and the Spartans won. On the third day he predicted, 'Death for all'. Before sunset Leonidas, Megistias and all the Spartan troops had been killed.

The seer Melampus of Pylos preferred to predict the future by listening to what animals were saying, claiming to be able to understand them. He was thrown in prison, but then predicted that the ceiling would collapse next day saying that he had overheard two termites talking about how they had munched through the rafters. The following day the ceiling did collapse.

From at least 500 BC the Roman Senate had possession of three ancient books written by Greek prophetesses of sibyls, known as the Sibylline Books. These books gave advice on what ceremonies should be carried out to gain the favour of the gods in different situations. The books were consulted only when some dire threat occurred, whether it was foreign invasion, famine or disease. The books were burned in AD 405 on the orders of the Christian general Stilicho.

THE BRAHAN SEER

Coinneach Odhar of the Mackenzie clan was born at Uig on the Scottish island of Lewis sometime around 1650. He claimed to be able to predict the future and to see far distant events by peering through a hole that had been naturally formed in a stone he picked up on the beach one day. He was hired by Kenneth MacKenzie, Earl of Seaforth, and lodged the Castle of Brahan.

The Brahan Seer predicted that, 'The day will come when a one-legged, fire-breathing giant shall come from Nigg.' In the late twentieth century, Nigg Bay became the site of a major construction site for the North Sea oil industry. The Ninian Central oil platform was built here. It has one main supporting leg and flares off excess gas in a giant flame.

The Brahan Seer predicted that, 'The day will come when ships will sail round the back of Tomnahurich Hill.' In 1822 the Caledonian Canal was built around the back of Tomnahurich Hill, allowing ships to take this route.

The Brahan Seer predicted that, 'The day will come when there are five bridges over the River Ness in Inverness and then there will be worldwide chaos.' The fifth bridge over the Ness in Inverness was completed on 20 August 1939. Less than two weeks later the Second World War began when Germany invaded Poland.

The Brahan Seer predicted that, 'The day will come when the MacKenzies of Fairburn shall lose their entire possessions; their castle will become uninhabited and a cow shall give birth to a calf in the uppermost chamber of the tower.' In 1851 a cow entered the ruined Fairburn Castle, struggled up to a loft where hay was being stored and gave birth to a calf.

Unfortunately for himself, the Brahan Seer one day peered through his stone and saw that the Earl of Seaforth was having an affair with a married French woman during a visit to Paris. The Earl's wife, who was at home in Brahan Castle, was furious and had the Brahan Seer murdered for bringing shame on her family – an outcome that the seer had not predicted.

OLD MOTHER SHIPTON

Ursula Southell was born in a cave near Knaresborough in Yorkshire in about 1488. She married Toby Shipton in 1512 and so in her old age was known as Old Mother Shipton. She was known locally for her skills with medicinal herbs and her occasional predictions of the future. In 1641 a book claiming to contain her collected predictions and prophecies was published. Some of Mother Shipton's prophecies were utterly obscure, such as:

> 'The land that rises from the sea
> Will be dry and clean and soft and free
> Of mankind's dirt and therefore be
> The source of man's new dynasty.'

One of Mother Shipton's rhymes runs:

> 'And Christian one fights Christian two
> And nations sigh, yet nothing do
> And yellow men great power gain
> From mighty bear with whom they've lain.'

Some think that the 'yellow men' refers to China and that the 'mighty bear' is Russia, but what the lines mean is unclear.

Mother Shipton foretold:

> 'A house of glass shall come to pass
> In England. But alas, alas
> A war will follow with the work
> Where dwells the Pagan and the Turk.'

This might refer to the Crystal Palace, built in 1851, and the Crimean War fought by Britain allied with Turkey against Russia in 1854.

Mother Shipton

The Yorkshire woman Old Mother Shipton has been credited with many accurate predictions.

Mother Shipton's prediction that, 'In water, iron, then shall float as easy as a wooden boat,' may have come true when iron ships began to be built.

Mother Shipton's prediction that, 'Gold shall be seen in stream and stone, in land that is yet unknown,' has been said to refer to the Californian gold rush of 1849.

Mother Shipton's prediction that, 'A carriage without horse will go,' is said to refer to the invention of the motor car.

Mother Shipton's prophecy that, 'Around the world men's thoughts will fly, quick as the twinkling of an eye,' has been interpreted as predicting the invention of radio, though more recently it has been taken as referring to the internet.

Mother Shipton said:

> 'When pictures seem alive with movements free,
> When boats like fishes swim beneath the sea,
> When men like birds shall scour the sky,
> Then half the world, deep drenched in blood shall die.'

This is said to refer to films, submarines, aircraft and the Second World War.

Mother Shipton's most famous prediction was that, 'The world to an end shall come, in eighteen hundred and eighty one.' However, the prophecy is not to be found in the book published in 1641; it was invented by journalist Charles Hindley in 1862.

NOSTRADAMUS

The most famous prophet of all time was the Frenchman Michel de Nostredame, better known by the Latin version of his name: Nostradamus. Born in 1503 to a grain merchant in St Rémy de Provence, Nostradamus travelled widely through Europe working as a plague doctor before he married a rich widow in 1547 and settled down back in Provence. He took up astrology and began casting horoscopes for local nobles and rich families, even being commissioned by Catherine de' Medici, Queen of France. He published three books of prophecies between 1555 and 1568. The prophecies were in the form of verses four lines long written in a bizarre mixture of French, Italian, Latin and Greek. Often all four languages were used in one verse. There were, in all, 942 verses, all of which are vague and obscure.

Verse 87 reads:

> 'Earth-shaking fires from the world's centre roar:
> Around new city is the earth a-quiver.
> Two nobles long shall wage a fruitless war,
> Arethusa will pour forth a new, red river.'

This has been taken to predict the Islamic terrorist attack on the World Trade Center in New York in 2001. The new city is said to be New York, the two nobles to be the Twin Towers and Arethusa (the name of a water nymph) to an anagram of The USA.

Nostradamus wrote, 'Beasts wild with hunger will cross the rivers, the greater part of the battlefield will be against Hister.

Nostradamus at his desk. The seer had travelled widely across Europe before marrying a rich widow and settling down to the business of making predictions.

He will drag the leader in a cage of iron, when the child of Germany observes no law.' This is often taken as a reference to Hitler, though as ever with Nostradamus, the match is not exact.

One of the most famous of the verses written by Nostradamus is:

> 'In the year 1999, and seven months,
> from the sky will come the great King of Terror.
> He will bring back to life the great king of the Mongols.
> Before and after War reigns happily.'

Needless to say, nothing much happened in August 1999 to match this dire warning.

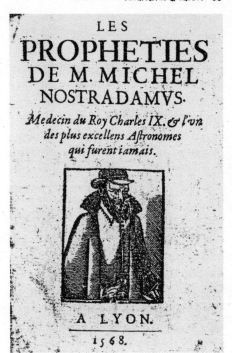

*The frontispiece of an
early edition
of the prophecies of
Nostradamus.*

Two quatrains are said to refer to Napoleon Bonaparte:

> 'An Emperor shall be born near Italy,
> Who shall cost the Empire dear,
> They shall say, with what people he keeps company
> He shall be found less a Prince than a butcher.'

and

> 'The great Empire will soon be exchanged for a small place.
> Which will soon begin to grow.
> A small place of tiny area in the middle of which
> He will come to lay down his scepter.'

Napoleon was born on Corsica, rose to be Emperor of France which he then led into a series of costly wars. He was dethroned and banished to Elba, then escaped to rule France again before being finally defeated and forced to abdicate.

SHIPPING PREDICTIONS

On 26 April 1909 the steamship *Waratah* called at Durban en route from Melbourne to Southampton. One of the 212 passengers on board, Claude Sawyer, left the ship even though he had booked a ticket all the way to England. He had experienced a dream of a man holding a bloodied sword which disturbed him deeply. The next day the *Waratah* left Durban and was never seen again, it simply vanished along with everyone on board and no trace was ever found.

In 1898 writer Morgan Robertson published a novel about a shipwreck. The fictional ship was named *Titan*, was the largest passenger liner afloat at 70,000 tons and sank on its maiden voyage after hitting an iceberg. In the book hundreds of lives were lost because the ship did not have enough lifeboats. In 1912 the real ship *Titanic* of 66,000 tons sank on its maiden voyage after hitting an iceberg. Hundreds of lives were lost because the ship did not have enough lifeboats.

In June 1858 American writer Mark Twain dreamed that he saw his elder brother Henry lying dead in a coffin with a posy of white lilies, and one red lily, on his chest. Two weeks later Twain received news that his brother had been killed when the Mississippi riverboat on which he was working had sunk near Memphis. Twain hurried to Memphis and found his brother's body in a coffin at the hospital. The body had on it a bunch of white lilies, with one red lily among them.

PREDICTING DISASTER

On the morning of 20 October 1966, nine-year-old Eryl Jones told her mother that she had had a very strange dream the night before. She said that in her dream she had gone to school, but that the school was not there. In its place there was a big, black thing. The following day a huge heap of coal waste slid down the hill above Aberfan and engulfed the school. Young Eryl was among the 140 dead.

On 6 December 1978 a man named Edward Pearson was arrested for boarding a train from Dundee to London without a ticket. When he appeared in court, Pearson gave his occupation as 'unemployed Welsh prophet'. He then insisted that it was vital that he went to London so that he could warn the government of an earthquake that was about to hit the city of Glasgow. There was much amusement in court. Two weeks later an earthquake hit Glasgow, the first in a hundred years.

In 1979 Spanish businessman Jaime Castell dreamed that he would die within three months. As a consequence he took out a life insurance policy for a huge sum of money, valid only for three months. Two months later Castell was driving to work when a car coming the other way went out of control, hit the kerb, flipped over and smashed into Castell's car, killing him instantly.

On 15 May 1979 and for the following nine nights Ohio office worker David Booth had the same identical nightmare. He dreamed seeing an American Airlines two-engined jet liner take off, then turn slowly over on to its back and crash into the ground in a ball of flames. After the fifth nightmare he phoned American Airlines, who logged the call and its details. On the day after the tenth nightmare an American Airlines DC-10, a two-engined jet airliner, was taking off from Chicago when it turned over on to its back and crashed in a ball of flames. There were no survivors.

GAMBLING PREDICTIONS

On 31 May 1933 John Williams of London dreamed that he was listening to the Derby horse race on the radio. The winner was a horse named Hyperion. Mr Williams was a Quaker and a firm opponent of gambling, so he did not put any money on the race. His neighbour, who had no such qualms, won a tidy sum when Hyperion did indeed with the Derby that year.

In December 1929 horse racing enthusiast Mr Freeman dreamed that he was held up while travelling to a race meeting at Lincoln. In his dream he arrived to be told that he had missed the first race, which had been won by a horse named Outram. In March the following year, Freeman was travelling to the races in Lincoln when he saw that a horse in the first race was named Outram. Unlike his dream, he arrived in time to place a bet, but just as in his dream Outram came first.

In 1768 in America, Christopher Knape dreamed that he had the winning numbers for the state lottery. He went out and bought a ticket, and duly won a substantial sum of money. Years later he had an identical dream and went out and bought a ticket, winning some money with two numbers matched. A third time he dreamt the numbers but when he went to buy his ticket he was informed they'd sold out – by the way, his numbers won again.

On nine occasions between 1946 and 1958 John Godley had a vivid dream in which he watched a horse win a race. Each time the dream turned out to be true, winning Godley substantial sums of money.

THE CURSES OF THE PHARAOHS

Ancient Egyptian tombs are often inscribed with curses that call down divine vengeance on anyone who tampers with the grave or the body buried within it.

The tomb of Ankhtifi, a government official of the Ninth Dynasty, has on its door the curse, 'To any man who does evil to this tomb, may the gods not accept your offering and may your heir not inherit.'

The Tenth Dynasty tomb of Khentika Ikhekhi has the wording, 'As for all men who shall enter this my tomb there will be judgment. An end shall be made for him. I shall seize his neck like a bird.'

The senior Egyptian archaeologist Zahi Hawass was a young historian when in the 1960s he excavated a tomb on which was written the curse, 'All people who enter this tomb who will make evil against this tomb – may the crocodile be against them in water, and snakes against them on land.' That night his cousin died, exactly one year later his uncle died and exactly a year after that his aunt died – after which the curse seems to have ended.

In 1922 the intact tomb of Pharaoh Tutankhamun was found by archaeologist Howard Carter, backed by Lord Carnarvon. Among the finds was a small tablet on which was carved, 'Death shall come on swift wings to him who disturbs the peace of the King.' Just a few weeks after opening Tutankhamun's tomb, Lord Carnarvon died of blood poisoning caused by an infected mosquito bite. Six months after Lord Carnarvon died, his brother Aubrey also died of blood poisoning, this time caused by an infected tooth.

American railway mogul George Jay Gould was among the first visitors to the tomb of Tutankhamun after it was opened. A few weeks later he developed a fever that no doctor could identify, and died six days later.

British diplomat working in Egypt, Sir Lee Stack, was another early visitor to the tomb of Tutankhamun. Less than a year later he was shot dead in the streets of Cairo by an unknown man.

Some years after discovering Tutankhamun's tomb, Carter gave his friend Sir Bruce Ingham a mummified hand with its wrist adorned with a scarab bracelet on which was carved, 'Cursed be he who moves my body. To him shall come fire, water and pestilence.' Less than three months later, Ingram's house burned down. It was only partly rebuilt when the remains were washed away by a flood.

VOODOO DOLLS

Around the Caribbean the large populations of imported slaves from Africa came from a mix of tribes and areas. In their new home these peoples gradually produced a new religion that was based on elements of the myths, religions and beliefs of the original tribes in Africa. The new religion took various forms in different areas, but they all go by one name: voodoo.

In Louisiana, voodoo dolls (properly called poppets) are used to send good luck, promote love or restore health more often than to inflict curses.

A voodoo doll, or poppet, can be used to inflict harm on a person. First the name of the person must be attached to the doll together with nail clippings, hair clippings or other such objects. Then pins should be pushed into the doll while curses are announced.

Louisiana voodoo teaches that a headache can be inflicted on a person by standing a voodoo doll or drawing of the person on its head.

ROMAN CURSES

The Romans and Greeks believed that they could inflict a curse using a curse tablet. This was a small sheet of lead on which the curse was written. The tablet was then folded or rolled up before being nailed to the walls of a temple or hidden in a tomb.

Curse tablets fixed to the walls of the goddess Minerva at Bath are almost all concerned with the same thing: cursing the thief who stole the person's clothes while they were swimming in the Roman bath.

A large proportion of Roman curse tablets begin or end with the word 'bazagra'. The word is entirely unknown in any other context and nobody knows what it means.

The curse tablets were usually addressed to a god, asking him to punish the person being cursed. The god mentioned most often was Charon, who worked the ferry that carried the souls of the dead over the River Styx to the next life.

Most of the curse tablets found in Athens are related to court cases. The most popular asks that a rival lawyer should become dizzy while giving a speech.

CURSED 13

According to Christian tradition, Judas Iscariot was the thirteenth man to sit down at the Last Supper with Jesus Christ. Judas went on to betray Jesus, so making the number 13 cursed for all time.

In Viking mythology, the god Loki was the thirteenth god to enter Valhalla. It was Loki's jealousy that caused the death of the beautiful Balder and so began Ragnarok, the Twilight of the Gods, when all creation was to be destroyed.

To the Maya, Aztec and other Central American peoples, each thirteenth day was endowed with a significance in an endlessly repeating 260-day cycle of good luck and bad luck.

Ancient Persians believed that each of the twelve signs of the Zodiac would dominate life on Earth for a thousand years. On the first day of the thirteenth thousand-year period, when no Zodiac sign would have precedence, the world would end.

FRIDAY 13TH

In medieval times Friday was considered an unlucky day to begin a journey, and Friday 13th doubly so. It is thought the modern unlucky status of Friday 13th derives from this belief.

It is estimated that around $800 million worth of business deals in the USA alone are delayed on each Friday 13th to be finalised on the following Monday.

Insurance companies have calculated that there are fewer claims for accidents on Friday 13th because people are more careful on those days.

The large asteroid Apophis is about 1,500ft in diameter. It is estimated to pass close to Earth on Friday 13 April 2029. If it were to hit Earth, Apophis would devastate about 5,000 square miles of territory if it hits land, or cause catastrophic tsunamis that might destroy vast areas of coastal regions if it strikes in the sea.

THE 27 CLUB

A large number of musicians have died at the age of twenty-seven. These include Robert Johnson, Jim Morrison, Brian Jones, Jimi Hendrix, Ron 'Pigpen' McKernan, Janis Joplin, Jonathan Brandis and Kurt Cobain.

CURSED JEWELS

The Hope Diamond is a blue diamond of 45.5 carats that is currently in the Smithsonian Museum in Washington DC. It is said to have been cursed when it was stolen from a Hindu temple where it served as the eye of an idol in about 1630. According to the legend, the thief was a Frenchman named Jean-Baptiste Tavernier, who died of fever soon after bringing the stone to France. King Louis XIV gave the stone to his mistress Madame de Montespan, who was promptly innocently embroiled in a poison scandal and exiled. The stone then passed to Finance Minister Nicolas Fouquet, who almost at once was arrested on false charges of embezzlement and imprisoned for life. The diamond then passed to Louis XVI who was executed, then to Princess de Lamballe who was raped and murdered, and to the Sultan Abdul Hamid who was forced to abdicate. The original large stone was then cut down to its current form by jeweller Jacques Colot, who was murdered by his son and the jewel was then sold by Simon Frankel, who went bankrupt. In 1839 the diamond was bought by Henry Hope, an Anglo-Dutch banker, who evaded the curse by not wearing it. The Hope family sold the jewel to Pierre Cartier in 1910, who sold it to an American jeweller who put it on display as the Cursed Hope Diamond. It was then bought, and worn without mishap, by socialite Evalyn McLean and in 1958 it was donated to the Smithsonian.

The Koh-i-Noor diamond is an Indian diamond of 105 carats that was discovered some time before the year 1200 in the Guntur region of India. It has a curse attached to it that states that, 'He who owns this diamond will own the world, but will also know all its misfortunes. Only God, or a woman, can wear it with impunity.' Several of its past owners have known great wealth and power, only to die in poverty or by violence. It is currently owned by the British royal family, only female members of which are allowed to use it.

The 190 carat Orloff Diamond is, like the Hope Diamond, said to have been stolen from a Hindu temple at some date in the past. It is said to bring bad luck to its owners. It is currently set into the sceptre of the Russian crown jewels.

DEADLY WATERS

Lough Gur in Ireland is said to demand a human death once every seven years. According to legend this belief originated in a custom of real human sacrifice in pagan times, but after Christianity stopped the sacrifices, the angry water goddess took to drowning her victims instead.

The Black Heddon Burn in Northumberland is said to have been cursed by a beautiful but malevolent witch named Silky who lived here some three centuries ago. Silky is said to demand a human life once every three years, and is widely blamed for the unusually large number of car crashes that occur on the bridge over the stream.

The river at Babinda in Queensland is said to have been cursed by an Aboriginal woman centuries ago. The beautiful young woman named Oolana was forced to marry a much older, but important, man by her family. She ran off with a handsome youngster at the first opportunity but when the couple were caught they she threw herself in to the river to drown. It is known that seventeen people have drowned swimming in the river since records began being kept in 1959.

TECUMSEH'S CURSE

In 1811 US soldier William Harrison defeated the forces of the Native American chief Tecumseh. He was cursed to enjoy great power and sudden death by Tecumseh's brother Tenskwatawa the Prophet. In 1840 Harrision became US President, but he died just thirty-one days later. From that date every US President elected in a year ending in 0 has died in office. The supposed curse was broken by Ronald Reagan, elected in 1980, who survived his two terms despite being shot by a would-be assassin.

6

POLTERGEISTS

The word 'poltergeist' comes form the German, meaning 'noisy ghost', but that does not even begin to do justice to the activities of this very disturbing form of paranormal activity. Poltergeists are, indeed, noisy – but they are also capable of moving objects, stealing things and making objects appear out of thin air. They seem to delight in causing as much nuisance as possible.

Poltergeists are much more sinister and destructive than any other form of paranormal activity. They come to create mayhem and mischief to homes, factories and offices. These are the ghosts that inspire film makers and novelists. A poltergeist will typically centre on a single person, termed 'the focus' by investigators. Focus persons are usually aged between fourteen and twenty-four and more often are female than male, though any person might find themselves subjected to a poltergeist visitation.

Most poltergeists start with unambitious acts such as making scratching noises or tapping on doors. Over a period of some weeks the poltergeist will progress to moving furniture, hammering on walls and stealing keys or other household objects – only to return them a few days later. In a small minority of cases the poltergeist will become hugely destructive, smashing windows, breaking furniture and setting fire to almost anything that will burn.

It is possible to communicate with poltergeists. Mostly this is done by asking it questions and waiting for a yes or no to be given in the form of knocks – two for 'yes' or one for 'no'. A few poltergeists learn how to write or even to speak. Invariably a poltergeist will claim a sensational and often grotesque origin for itself, and always one that fits in with local beliefs. In centuries gone by a poltergeist might claim to be a fairy, devil or witch; in Arabian countries they claim to be a 'djinn' (genie) and in modern Western countries they usually lay claim to be a ghost of a murder victim, or a murderer. Where such claims can be checked they invariably turn out to be untrue.

Not all poltergeists perform the same range of antics. One poltergeist may do nothing more than throw stones, another concentrate on moving kitchen utensils about; a third might ignore such mundane tricks and instead concentrate on hugely destructive acts that inflict physical injury on the victims. Only a very few poltergeists exhibit the full range of possible manifestations. Of this small number one of the most famous was the Bell Witch, so called because it plagued a family named Bell and claimed to be a witch. Active on a small farm in Tennessee during the 1820s, the Bell Witch would become a classic of the paranormal.

Investigators are deeply divided over what causes a poltergeist visitation. Taken at face value, a poltergeist would seem to be some form of invisible spiritual entity possessed of great power and, often, deep malevolence. Whether this entity should be considered to be a demon, a ghost, a djinn, a fairy or some other being is a matter of opinion and most researchers prefer not to give a definitive opinion on a matter that is probably beyond solving.

However, many poltergeist cases seem to indicate that the presence of a disembodied entity may not be the correct explanation. Very often outbreaks of paranormal violence seem to be triggered by events that happen to the focus – an argument with a family member for instance. This would indicate that the focus may be playing an unconscious role in events. Many researchers believe that the focus person is actually creating the poltergeist visitation through some unknown form of psychokinetic energy, allowing them to move objects by the power of thought alone. It is thought that the poltergeist activity is an unconscious lashing out by the focus person.

Others think that it is not so much the focus person causing the events, but the people around them. Most poltergeists usually occur in a place where a small group of people spend long hours together: family homes and workplaces are the favoured haunts of poltergeists. It may be that a complex interplay between different individuals is needed to cause a poltergeist visitation.

In the final analysis, nobody really knows what causes a poltergeist to manifest itself. Sceptics argue that all supposed manifestations are capable of explanation in conventional terms. Objects that are supposedly taken by a poltergeist and then returned are said to have been simply mislaid, unexplained noises are put down to rats or faulty central heating and anything that cannot be readily explained is brushed off as being a trick perpetrated by the teenager who is the supposed focus. Such rationalisation of events may seem perfectly valid from the security of a place remote in place and time from the poltergeist, but for those subjected to the full panoply of a destructive haunting the events are very, very real indeed.

STONE-THROWERS

Helpidius was the personal physician of the Gothic monarch Theodoric the Great in the 510s. For several months one summer his home in Rome became famous for the 'flying stones' which cascaded down on to its roof from unseen origins.

In 858 a farmer near Bingen, Germany, found himself hit by stones thrown by unseen hands whenever he went outside. He believed that a demon was attacking him and a priest was sent from Mainz to get rid of the assailant. As the priest began the ceremony an avalanche of stones struck him from behind. He fled.

On 29 November 1591 the Oxfordshire home of the Lee family was subjected to a barrage of stones. The rocks varied in size from a small pebble up to 22lbs in weight. Each stone arrived in identical fashion, falling to the floor with a thud as if dropped from ceiling height. There were, however, no holes in the ceilings and nobody in sight who could have thrown the stones. After this initial barrage, stones continued to appear from nowhere inside the house off and on for some weeks. Days might pass without a stone being seen, then a dozen would appear all at once. The eldest son, twenty-two-year-old George, died in May 1592 after which the stones stopped appearing.

On 11 June 1685 a poltergeist, called a demon at the time, began an assault on the home of George Walton in Portsmouth, New England. A shower of several hundred pebbles began falling on to the roof of the house with a loud rattling sound. The family went outside to find themselves deluged by stones. Several people were hit by the falling stones, but they suffered no injury as the stones bounced off harmlessly. The pebbles seemed to be appearing out of thin air several feet above the house. The stone shower stopped, but repeated itself a few days later and continued to manifest itself several times until about November, when the attacks ceased.

In 1935 a poltergeist attacking a house in Eland Road, in the Battersea area of London, began by throwing small pieces of coal on to the roof of a conservatory. It then threw some pennies, followed by more coal and some stones. Over the coming weeks it is estimated that more than 500 stones and bits of coal appeared apparently from nowhere.

A variation on throwing stones was shown by the famous Bell Witch. This poltergeist took to throwing sticks and cut logs. The pieces of wood usually came flying out of a thicket beside the road that led to the Bell Farm and were thrown at anyone walking or riding along the road.

ODD OBJECTS

In 1889 a poltergeist that infested a Quebec farm owned by the Dagg family developed a fascination with money. It moved cash from one place to another, even throwing a five-dollar bill into a fireplace on one occasion.

In 1658 at Loddington in Northamptonshire a poltergeist in the home of the Stiff family became obsessed with bread. It would hurl bread loaves around the kitchen and on one occasion caused a loaf to dance back and forth along the table in front of the family.

Baking in the kitchen, here seemingly unhindered by poltergeists.

In 1966 a poltergeist played about with the plumbing in the home of the Pritchard family in Pontefract, Yorkshire. If the kitchen tap was turned on, the toilet would flush. If the toilet was flushed the bath taps would gush. Pools of water appeared from nowhere on the kitchen floor.

In 1887 the Foster family of Appleby, Cumbria, were plagued by a poltergeist which seemed obsessed with an old pram that was kept in a store room. Although it threw stones, smashed windows and shifted furniture about, the poltergeist moved the pram more often than anything else. It once pushed the pram around for more than half an hour.

In 1996 the Kirk family of Pudsey, Yorkshire, were host to a poltergeist that was fascinated by electrical appliances. The kettle, television, lights, iron and other objects were switched on or off at frequent intervals over a period of some months. At first the Kirks called in electricians, but later just accepted the activity.

A poltergeist that afflicted a blacksmith's workshop in Vienna in July 1906 took a liking to a large pair of compasses. It would move them around so that they could not be found and delighted in whisking them out of reach of whoever was using them. On one occasion the compasses were used by the poltergeist to smack an apprentice over the head.

In 1960 Scottish schoolgirl Virginia Campbell became the focus of a poltergeist. The entity caused her school desk to fly open, to levitate and to walk about the classroom.

In 1967 the Tropication Warehouse in Miami, Florida, was targeted by a poltergeist that seemed to take a dislike to the cheap tourist souvenirs that were stored there. After getting off to a slow start, the poltergeist increased its attacks until it was smashing more than a dozen ornaments each day.

In 2002 the Brushmaker's Arms pub at Upham, Hampshire, had trouble with beer glasses. They would be found in the morning scattered all over the bar room, but none of them were broken. It was as if unseen hands had picked them up and carefully placed them about the pub.

The poltergeist that afflicted a Hertfordshire couple seemed to become obsessed with money. Whenever the wife put money in her purse or handbag it would vanish, only to reappear somewhere about the house. Several times she went to a shop to purchase something only to find that she had no money. Once she was fined for travelling on a train without a ticket or the money to buy one.

A poltergeist of the 1980s in a heating shop habitually moved the shop telephone from the desk to sit in the middle of the floor. More than once a customer tripped over it.

DANGEROUS POLTERGEISTS

In August 1878 the Teed family of Amherst, Nova Scotia, were visited by a poltergeist that seemed to have a grudge against a young sister of Mrs Teed, eighteen-year-old Esther Cox. When the poltergeist first arrived, Esther would turn bright red, her hair would stand on end and her body swell up to twice its normal size. The poltergeist later set fire to several objects around the house, including Esther's dress, a stack of firewood, a tablecloth and basket of laundry.

The Bell Witch claimed responsibility for the death of farmer John Bell on 20 December 1820. Mr Bell had not enjoyed the best of health for some time when, on 19 December suffered some sort of seizure and was put to bed. Next morning he was found to be dead and a small bottle of liquid was found by the bedside. The poltergeist gleefully announced that it had given Bell some of the liquid to drink and so had killed him. The liquid was tested on a cat, which promptly died.

In November 1761 a poltergeist came to the house of the Giles family near Bristol. It began with strange noises, progressed to moving furniture but in April the following year, events turned nasty. Molly Giles, aged thirteen, was subjected to what looked like bites from a human which left behind painful red marks and bruises. After this had gone on for some time, she began to be stabbed by pins that materialised from nowhere and plunged into her arms and legs. Finally, shallow but very painful knife cuts manifested themselves. The poltergeist then began to speak, claiming to be a demonic familiar spirit sent by a witch. Soon afterwards Mr Giles fell ill and died, and the poltergeist claimed responsibility. Mrs Giles then called in a local witch who undertook a number of rituals in the house. The poltergeist was experienced no more.

LURID CLAIMS

A poltergeist that plagued a convent in France in 1524 claimed to be a novice nun named Alix de Telieux who had left the convent four years earlier. It said that since leaving, Alice had stolen jewels, indulged in bizarre sexual adventures and taken to heavy drinking and gambling. The lurid tales shocked the nuns, but could not be proved to be true or false.

In 1612 a poltergeist plagued the house of François Perrault in Mâcon, France. It claimed that Perrault's father had been murdered by a neighbour, that Perrault's kitchen maid was a witch, that a neighbour was committing adultery and a host of other accusations – none of which turned out to be true.

In 1851 a poltergeist attacked the home of the Revd Eliakim Phelps in Stratford, Connecticut. It delighted in removing clothes from wardrobes and either throwing them about the room or laying them out as if a person was inside them asleep. The poltergeist claimed to be the spirit of a Frenchman who had been condemned to hell by God. It poured out a stream of tales of the wicked crimes it had committed when alive, but refused to give details – such as names and places – that could be checked out.

In 1932 a poltergeist became active in a farmhouse on the Isle of Man owned by the Irving family. It claimed to be the ghost of a mongoose and said its name was Gef.

GOSSIPING POLTERGEISTS

The poltergeist that afflicted a farm at Bingen am Rhein in 856 began its activities with stone-throwing and moving objects, but it soon learned to talk. The poltergeist accused the man who owned the farm of having an affair with the teenage daughter of the farm foreman. The claims were lurid, detailed and scandalous. The voice of the poltergeist would follow the unfortunate man to market, to church and elsewhere to announce his supposed sexual misdemeanours to anyone who would listen.

When focus teenager Betsy Bell began seeing a local farmer, Joshua Gardner, the Bell Witch poltergeist took a dislike to the young man. The poltergeist would give the Bell family a running commentary on what the two youngsters were doing when they went for a walk or spent some time alone together. When they kissed, when they held hands and what they said were all passed on in graphic detail. Eventually the couple split up.

In 1190 a poltergeist visited the home of Stephen Wiriet in Pembroke. It began by throwing handfuls of dirt around, but then produced a voice. Anyone who came to visit the Wiriet household would be accused of theft, jealousy, adultery, lust, greed and other sins. Very often the poltergeist seemed to be repeating local gossip, but at other times appeared to be simply making things up.

ENTER THE PRIEST

Many families afflicted by a poltergeist turn to religion for help. Unfortunately this usually has little effect.

At Jaboticabal in Brazil in 1965 the local priest was summoned to bless a house afflicted by a stone-throwing poltergeist.

The priest had no sooner finished his ceremony and left the house when there came a loud crash. The family found that no fewer than 312 small stones had fallen into their house. A few days later the poltergeist methodically smashed every piece of crockery in the house.

In April 1975 the Marcos family of São Paolo, Brazil, called in a priest to get rid of a poltergeist that was throwing stones, cutting furniture and starting fires. The priest came with a colleague to carry out a ceremony of exorcism. The two clerics had barely begun before they were bombarded with a rain of pebbles.

HELPFUL POLTERGEISTS

The Bell Witch played many cruel tricks on teenage Betsy Bell, the focus of the manifestations, but could also prove useful. When neighbours came round to help celebrate Betsy's birthday, the poltergeist materialised a large basket filled with oranges, bananas, grapes and nuts. The fruit and basket materialised from nowhere on to the table.

The poltergeist that afflicted a shop in Cardiff in 1980 mostly threw stones, but sometimes produced other objects. When shopowner John said he had to go to fetch a pencil to write down a customer's order, a pen and pad of pencil were thrown at him. When a shop worker told a colleague that he was a bit short of money, three coins fell to the floor – but they were pre-decimal pennies, and so quite useless for a trip to the pub.

The poltergeist that took up residence in a furniture shop in York in the 1970s spent most of its time moving furniture about, sometimes piling chairs on top of each other. However, it also regularly caused coins to appear from nowhere and then threw them at customers.

THE POLICE INVESTIGATE

In 1981 residents of four houses in Thornton Road, Birmingham, called in the police to investigate smashed roof tiles and windows caused by stones being thrown at the houses at night. Chief Inspector Turley began by putting a constable on watch, but when this sentinel saw nothing, more men were drafted in. Finally round-the-clock vigils were carried out by policemen equipped with night-vision equipment. No human culprit was ever found, though the breakages continued.

'We are completely baffled,' announced Turley. 'We have tried everything we know without being able to find out who is doing this.'

One Monday in September 1937 Mr Cappy Ricks found his home in Mauritius was being struck by stones thrown by unseen assailants. He sent for the police. They arrived, but no further stones were thrown that day. On Tuesday more stones were thrown, this time they also appeared inside the house, dropping as if through a hole in the roof. On Wednesday the stones became bigger, one weighed 6lb, and the movements were more violent with pieces of crockery being broken by the stones. The police were called again and constables stationed outside to catch any intruders. On Thursday the police and the poltergeist returned – this time along with a crowd of several hundred onlookers. By lunchtime over 100 stones had appeared inside the house or been thrown at it, more crockery was broken, all the curtains had been ripped down and the furniture tossed about into chaos. Neither the police nor the crowd outside could see anyone responsible. That evening the poltergeist ceased activity and never returned.

The sheriff of Big Bear City, California, was called to a house that was being pelted with dozens of stones by an unseen assailant. When he arrived in his car, he got out to be immediately pelted with over 40 pebbles, up to 10oz in weight.

'What was odd,' the sheriff later reported, 'was that the rocks did not make enough noise. The damage to the car was much less than it should have been considering the size of the rocks.'

In December 2008 the home of Ratan Das and his family in Kolkata, India, was visited by a poltergeist that targeted the teenage daughter Rima and her school books. Police Inspector Sukumar was called to view the damage. He decided that neighbouring children jealous of Rima's success at school were to blame. He hid police constables in the house garden with orders to arrest any teenagers seen approaching the house. No teenagers were seen, but the mayhem continued for seven days before stopping as soon as it began.

A policeman who came to investigate odd goings-on at Shattock Farm north of Glasgow in 1878 responded in a very firm way. The policemen sat down at the kitchen table to make notes and interview the family and workers. Suddenly a loaf of bread rose out of the bread bin, floated gently across the kitchen and came to rest on the table in front of him. He arrested everyone in the room, 'just in case.'

SEEING THE POLTERGEIST

Nearly all poltergeists are invisible. They can be heard and their antics are all too visible, but the poltergeist itself is never seen. In a very few cases, however, an apparition does materialise. It is not clear if the apparition is the actual poltergeist or simply another trick.

Samuel Jones of Runcorn suffered a poltergeist in his family home which threw stones, hid objects and moved furniture. The apparition was, however, seen at the farm where he worked. The farmer saw a shapeless black cloud move slowly across his farmyard and enter the pigsty, where the pigs were soon to die of a mysterious ailment. The black cloud was seen several times at the farm, always when Jones was at work and once it followed him down a track.

During a poltergeist attack in Epworth, Yorkshire, (that was blamed on witches as it took place in 1716) an odd creature was seen several times. Emily, the girl who kept a diary of events, recorded, 'It was seen by my mother under my sister's bed. Like a badger only without any head that was discernable.' Some days later, 'the same creature sat by the dining room fire one evening. When our man went into the room it run up by him through the hall and under the stairs.'

The poltergeist activity that plagued the Berini family of Grant, New York State, was accompanied by the apparition of a dwarf man dressed in a black suit and wearing outsized black shoes. The dwarf made a series of lewd suggestions to Mrs Berini whenever the two met.

The Greenfield family of London's West Norwood suffered a fairly typical poltergeist visitation that lasted about six months. Towards the end of the visitation the figure of a tall man with long grey hair was seen several times in the house.

BLOODY POLTERGEISTS

In St Quentin, France, in 1986 a poltergeist spent several days splashing blood on the bed sheets and bedroom carpet.

When Mrs Winston of Atlanta, Georgia, opened her bathroom door in 1987 she found the floor swimming in blood. She collected some and sent it for analysis. It turned out to be human blood of type O – Mrs Winston and her husband were both type A.

In March 1985 a poltergeist in Abidjan, Ivory Coast, introduced a new note of horror when it began leaving bloody footprints around the house. Things got worse when it filled all the pans in the kitchen with blood. The crescendo came when fountains of blood gushed from the walls. Unsurprisingly the family fled the house at this point.

POLTERGEISTS ON FIRE

In the early months of 1905 a poltergeist attacked White Farm near Louth in Lincolnshire. Among other activities, the poltergeist killed over 200 chickens by snapping their necks at night. It then set fire to the dress of a servant girl, inflicting injuries that put her in hospital for two weeks.

In 1989 thirteen-year-old Sara Cardoso of Rio de Janeiro became the focus for a poltergeist after having a vivid dream in which the Devil said that he was coming to collect her. Over the next couple of months more than 50 small fires broke out spontaneously. The most destructive blaze destroyed all the clothes in a wardrobe, while the most mysterious came when a wet towel caught fire amid a sheet of steam and the most dramatic came when a mattress exploded as if filled with gunpowder.

In 1695 the home of stonemason Andrew Mackie at Ringcroft, Scotland, was plagued by a poltergeist that scattered burning wisps of straw about. Among other damage, the sheets of a bed were set on fire while two of the Mackie children were sleeping in it and the thatched roof of a sheep shed was set ablaze.

In August 1856 Mrs Moulton of Bedford smelled burning and found the mattress in the spare room ablaze. A few minutes later a nearby blanket began smouldering, followed by a dress inside a closed wardrobe. Next day a pile of bed linen caught fire while the housemaid stood nearby. When the maid went to report the strange event to Mrs Moulton a cushion on the sofa on which Mrs Moulton was sitting burst into flames.

More than twenty-four similar blazes broke out that day. Mr Moulton came home next day from a business trip and the strange fires ceased.

During seven days in December 1891 no fewer than forty-five fires broke out in the home of Robert Dawson of Toronto. In each case the flames began within a few feet of fourteen-year-old Jennie Bramwell, an orphan working in the Dawson household as a maid. After the terrified Bramwell left to live in an orphanage the fires ceased.

In 1982 a poltergeist visitation afflicting the Newman family of Sheffield, Yorkshire, reached a dramatic conclusion. The family were all asleep upstairs when the poltergeist began hammering on the walls and doors, succeeding in waking everybody up. Mr Newman opened his bedroom door to check if the children were alright, when he saw smoke gushing up from downstairs. He bundled his family out of an upstairs window to escape via a flat roof. The house burned down, and Mr Newman credited the poltergeist with saving their lives. Whether it had also started the fire was unclear.

In August 1982 Scottish teenager Carole Compton, working as a nanny in Italy, was arrested and put in prison. The arrest followed a series of poltergeist activity in the Tonti family where Compton worked. The assorted incidents had culminated in the bed of three-year-old Agnese Tonti being set on fire. The Tonti grandmother had called the police, accused Compton of being a witch and demanded her instant arrest. The police found no evidence that Compton had been responsible and forensic experts were at a total loss, but the influential Tonti family insisted that 'the witch' be punished, so Compton was charged with attempted murder of young Agnese and with arson. Her trial took place in December 1983 by which time she had been in prison for sixteen months. She was found guilty of arson and sentenced to sixteen months in prison, meaning that she was released at once.

7

PARANORMAL HUMANS

For most humans, everyday life is a matter of dealing with the world through the five commonly accepted senses: sight, hearing, touch, taste and smell. These provide us with all that we know of the world about us. Using them we can get up in the morning, prepare breakfast, go to work, build relationships with our fellow humans and generally have rich, varied and fulfilling lives.

However, there are a small number of people who would seem to have other senses than the usual five. These come in many and varied forms. Some people claim to be able to read the minds of others. A few individuals say that they can 'see' what is happening many miles away. The ability to move objects using only mind power is another ability claimed by some. Finding water by dowsing, healing by the laying on of hands or sending messages to another by thought power are other powers that have been claimed by many individuals over the years.

Widely varied though these claimed abilities may be, they do share one feature in common: there is no known mechanism by which they could be achieved. Very often the people claiming to have the power or gift in question cannot explain how they do it. More than one person, when asked how they managed to perform a particular feat, would reply that it just sort of happens to them.

Indeed, this feeling that a sense or power of this kind is essentially beyond the control of the person involved is very widespread. People claiming telepathic powers will report that they just suddenly know that something is true or has taken place, but will not be able to explain how they know this fact. The ability to control such senses is rare, but not unknown. Some such people seek to make money from their claimed gifts, others seek to help others.

However, the extra senses are not always as useful as might be supposed. They can be frustratingly vague while at the same time being accurate. One famous case from the 1930s came when a woman claimed that her missing son had been murdered by having his skull smashed with a blunt instrument and the body had been dumped in a dark, confined space under the ground that was very wet. When the missing young man was eventually found, he was discovered to have been murdered with a blow from a hammer and his body disposed of by being pushed into a disused well. The mother had been absolutely correct in every detail, even to the clothes that the son had been wearing when killed, but the description of the body's hiding place had not been precise enough to help police find the body. After all, there are many thousands of damp, underground places in England. The police cannot be expected to search them all.

An interesting facet of these gifts is that they almost invariably decrease or disappear when subjected to scientific investigation. Sceptics would argue that this indicates that the supposed extra senses or powers are non-existent. They would suggest that knowledge gained supposedly from reading minds is, in fact, merely coincidence or an educated guess. Certainly some charlatans have been known to engage in a process known as 'cold reading' and than to pass it off as some form of psychic ability.

This cold reading is a technique often used by stage magicians to mimic the ability to mind read. At its simplest it relies upon the law of averages, allowing the supposed mind-reader to tell a person that, 'I sense that your father passed away owing to problem in the chest or abdomen.' If the person having their mind read is over the age of fifty it is more likely than not that their father will have died and since most men die of chest or abdomen problems there is a good chance the statement will be correct. Skilled practitioners are able to gauge a person's reactions by their body language or eye contact, allowing them to pick up on a fact and home in on it as if reading the person's mind.

Despite such sceptical responses, it remains a fact that a large number of people are able to display gifts and senses that are far beyond the limits of coincidence or averages. They genuinely seem to display abilities that are beyond most humans. Quite how these senses operate, and the degree to which they can be relied upon, are currently the subject of study by many psychical researchers around the world.

ELECTRIC PEOPLE

In 1887 Caroline Clare of Ontario fell seriously ill. When she recovered she had become a human dynamo. She gave electric shocks to anyone who touched her and metal objects became magnetically charged if she held them for any amount of time. The strange gifts faded away after six months.

In 1967 Brian Clements was reported to the British national press for his amazing build-ups of static electricity. For no obvious reason his body was accumulating enormously powerful charges that discharged themselves with a painful and sometimes visible flash of lightning every few minutes.

For ten weeks from 15 January 1846 Angelique Cottin of Normandy not only displayed powerful magnetic powers, but could control them at will. She had only to wave a hand for a metal object either to leap away from her or fly into her hand. She lifted a 60lb weight by holding her hand above it. She was

*For several weeks Angelique Cottin displayed strong magnetic
powers, but they vanished as suddenly as they came.*

studied by eminent doctors who found no sign of trickery. The
powers vanished abruptly.

In 1890 Ann Abbott of Georgia seemed to become a powerful
magnet. She went on the stage and made a considerable sum of
money before her powers vanished as mysteriously as they had
appeared.

The notes of a rural doctor from St Urbain, France, for 1969
record the birth of a peculiar baby. It gave electric shocks to
anyone who touched it. Sadly the infant did not survive long,
proving to be sickly.

In 1938 Antoine Timmer found that she had suddenly become
magnetic. Iron and steel cutlery, scissors and other household
objects stuck to her and could be removed only with some effort.
The strange phenomenon lasted a few weeks, then faded.

In 1890 Louis Hamburger of Maryland suddenly found his hands behaved like powerful magnets. He could pick up cutlery, needles and other metal objects with his finger tips. He demonstrated his gifts by grasping a glass jar of iron filings and causing the filings to leap to the parts touched by his hands.

On the evening of 25 January 1837 Mrs Hosford of New Hampshire fell ill. After a night of fever she recovered to find that she gave powerful electric shocks to anyone she touched, and suffered them herself when touching metal. Sparks up to an inch long could be generated every 20 seconds. The electric shocks faded after six weeks.

In 1889 Frank McKinstry of Missouri found that he charged up with electricity overnight. Every morning he had to discharge the build-up by touching a metal rod – invariably unleashing a bright flash and experiencing great pain.

HELPING THE POLICE

In October 1888 English psychic Robert James Lees was on a London bus when he suddenly 'knew' that one of his fellow passengers was a murderer. He followed the man to his home at 74 Brook Street, which revealed him to be Sir William Gull, a well-known doctor. Lees was convinced that Gull was the serial killer then stalking London who had become known as Jack the Ripper. He went to the police, who discovered that Gull had recently begun acting strangely and flying into uncharacteristic violent rages. Soon afterwards Gull's family had him committed to an asylum, after which the killings stopped.

In October 1978 a seven-year-old boy named Carl Carter vanished from his Los Angeles home. A local clairvoyant had a vision showing the boy being strangled by a man. She contacted the police and gave them a description that matched that of a family friend, Butch Memro. Memro was questioned,

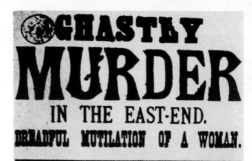

GHASTLY MURDER

IN THE EAST-END.

DREADFUL MUTILATION OF A WOMAN.

Capture : Leather Apron

Another murder of a character even more diabolical than that perpetrated in Back's Row, on Friday week, was discovered in the same neighbourhood, on Saturday morning. At about six o'clock a woman was found lying in a back yard at the foot of a passage leading to a lodging-house in a Old Brown's Lane, Spitalfields. The house is occupied by a Mrs. Richardson, who lets it out to lodgers, and the door which admits to this passage, at the foot of which lies the yard where the body was found, is always open for the convenience of lodgers. A lodger named Davis was going down to work at the time mentioned and found the woman lying on her back close to the flight of steps leading into the yard. Her throat was cut in a fearful manner. The woman's body had been completely ripped open and the heart and other organs laying about the place, and portions of the entrails round the victim's neck. An excited crowd gathered in front of Mrs. Richardson's house and also round the mortuary in old Montague Street, whither the body was quickly conveyed. As the body lies in the rough coffin in which it has been placed in the mortuary - the same coffin in which the unfortunate Mrs. Nicholls was first placed - it presents a fearful sight. The body is that of a woman about 45 years of age. The height is exactly five feet. The complexion is fair, with wavy brown hair; the eyes are blue, and two lower teeth have been knocked out. The nose is rather large and prominent.

A poster announcing a murder by Jack the Ripper. An English psychic was convinced that he identified the killer even as the murders continued.

broke down and confessed to the murder and that of two other young boys.

The limits of psychic help were shown in 1979 when clairvoyant Doris Stokes tried to help the police find the Yorkshire Ripper, a serial killer murdering women in northern England. She said that the killer had a scar below his left eye, was named Ronnie, had a surname beginning with M, lived in a street named Berwick and had a recently deceased mother named Molly. When caught, the killer was Peter Sutcliffe, who did not have a mother named Molly, did not have a scar and did not live in a street named Berwick.

In October 1979 clairvoyant Nella Jones also produced a vision of the Yorkshire Ripper. She said that he lived in Bradford at a house no. 6, was named Peter and worked as a lorry driver for a company the name of which began with the letter C. She was later proved to be correct in every detail.

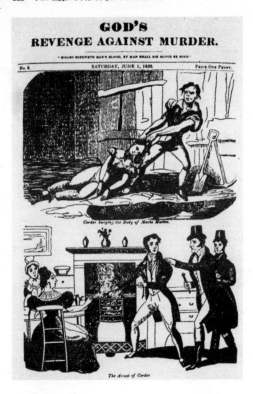

William Corder is shown in a contemporary engraving killing his lover Maria Marten and being arrested. It was because of a vision by the victim's mother that the murder was uncovered.

In 1827 Maria Marten of Polstead, Suffolk, had a child by local farmer's son William Corder. As a result Corder proposed that the couple move away to Ipswich and get married. The couple left Polstead and vanished. Maria's mother then had a series of vivid dreams in which she saw her daughter dead and buried in the Red Barn, a nearby farm building. The barn floor was excavated and Maria's body found exactly as her mother said. Corder was located living under an assumed name, tried and executed.

When Dennis Prado went missing in California the police failed to find any trace of him. His family then contacted psychic Annette Martin who 'saw' that Prado had gone for a walk, only to drop dead of a sudden stroke. The body, she said, was hidden in bushes. Using a map Martin pinpointed the spot and two men set off to investigate. They found the body almost at once.

METAL-BENDING

The paranormal bending of small metal objects, such as cutlery or pins, had long been a feature of poltergeist activity. It became a separate phenomenon when Uri Geller began bending metal by apparently paranormal means in the early 1970s. Nobody was ever able to find evidence that Geller was faking the phenomenon.

In 1975 the journal *Nature* printed a paper by Professor J.B. Hasted in which he claimed to have produced paranormal metal-bending results. Pieces of metal were fitted with stress gauges and those trying to bend them were not allowed to touch them, but the metal bent anyway.

Swedish investigator Dr Georg Wikman tested French metal-bender Jean Pierre Girard by holding up a 3-inch screw sealed inside a plastic tube. Girard stared at the tube, without touching it and within 15 seconds the screw had bent almost double.

By the later 1970s several stage magicians had developed techniques for bending cutlery that mimicked the apparently paranormal events. This did not disprove the paranormal claims, but did cause the media to lose interest.

APPORTS

An apport is an object that appears from nowhere. They are generally quite small objects, but sometimes may be much larger. They are most often reported during poltergeist visitations, but some people claim to be able to produce them.

During the 1980s London medium Paul McElhoney produced fresh flowers apparently out of thin air. Usually, but not always, the flowers appeared from his mouth.

In 1880 medium Madame d'Esperance produced a 6-foot tall golden lily plant, complete with blooms, in an empty vase that she did not touch during the séance. At a later séance it vanished as mysteriously as it had appeared.

In the 1860s medium Agnes Nichols (better known by her later married name of Guppy) produced fruit and vegetables to order. Among the objects that appeared on a table in the darkened séance room were: oranges, white grapes, black grapes, apples, walnuts, damsons, figs, onions, peaches, almonds, dates, potatoes, pears and even crystallised greengages.

When asked to produce an apport in 1893, medium Mrs Everitt refused saying, 'I don't approve of bringing them as they are generally stolen.'

In 1904 Italian investigator Ernesto Bozzano tested a medium by asking for a piece of iron pyrites. A small amount of powdered pyrites appeared. When Bozzano got home he found that a piece of pyrites in his desk had been broken in two and one piece was missing.

In the 1930s former miner Jack Webber produced a number of apports at séances. At one séance he was searched and tied up by a policeman, then produced two small Egyptian ornaments.

Indian guru and mystic Sathya Sai Baba is considered by some Hindus to be a living divine avatar. Among the various miracles claimed to have been accomplished by him are the apports of statues, photographs, Indian pastries (both hot and cold), food (hot, cold, solid and fluid), out-of-season fruits, new banknotes, pendants, necklaces, watches and rings.

HUMAN GLOW WORMS

In 1934 Anna Monaro of Pirano, Italy, began to suffer much worse attacks of asthma than she did normally. Her husband noticed that as she slept, Monaro glowed gently with a bluish light around her torso. The doctor confirmed the glow and sent for a senior physician who studied the glow and announced that it was caused by 'magnetic and electrical organisms in the woman's body'. After several weeks the glow subsided, as did the severe asthma attacks.

In September 1869 an American woman, who preferred to remain anonymous, was reported by her doctor to have a luminous toe. The fourth toe on the woman's right foot gave off a greenish light at night. Over the following few days the glow spread across the entire foot and up beyond the ankle. It gradually faded and within a month was gone.

In 1608 Tobias da Ponte went to visit his priest, Bernardino Realini. He entered the priest's house and found him apparently unconscious but radiating a bright light from his face and hands. Other parishioners also saw the light of the priest over the next few weeks.

EXTRASENSORY PERCEPTION (ESP) IN BUSINESS

In 1944 US businessman Conrad Hilton placed a sealed bid of $165,000 for the Stevens Corporation. Then, just before the sealed auction ended, he had a strong urge to up the bid to $180,000, which he did. He won the auction by a margin of just $200.

On 12 April 1906 US financier Jesse Livermore was on holiday when he felt an overwhelming urge to sell the shares he held in the highly profitable Union Pacific Railroad. He finally found a telegraph office and sent a message to his stockbroker. Six days later the San Francisco Earthquake struck, destroying huge quantities of Union Pacific track and rolling stock. The company's stock price plummeted.

Charles Wilson, the man who steered Holiday Inn to international success, used to commission reports on possible sites for new hotels. Having chosen likely sites he made a final decision by going to the site and smelling the air. He said he invariably got a hunch as to whether or not to build on the site.

Herbert Raiffe was a cuddly toy manufacturer when, in 1971, he had a sudden feeling that pandas would sell well the following year. The hunch proved to be so intense that he ordered his factory to concentrate on pandas over teddy bears. A few weeks later US President Richard Nixon visited China and was presented with two pandas to take back to America. Demand for cuddly toy pandas boomed, and Raiffe made a fortune.

ESP UNDER TEST

Polish engineer Stephan Ossowiecki claimed to be able to read any piece of paper sealed in an envelope. To test Ossowiecki, Eric Dingwall drew a flag and a wine bottle and wrote 'Aug 22. 1923' on a sheet of paper, then sealed it in an envelope, sealed *that* in an envelope and that in a third then posted it to a colleague with instructions to show it to Ossowiecki. Ossowiecki held the envelope for 5 seconds, then drew a flag and bottle adding '22 1923'.

Señora Zierold of Mexico claimed to be able to pick up past events simply by holding an object. Dr Pagenstecher tested this in 1923 by giving her an object, a piece of string, sent to him by a friend in Germany, the history of which he did not know. Zierold said that she saw an open field on a foggy day with men carrying guns, then a ball of fire fell from the sky and killed some of the men. The string turned out to have been the string that held the identity disk worn by the German colleague when he had fought in the First World War.

In 1930 Dr J. Rhine tested the ability of Hubert Pearce to identify cards by dealing a pack of shuffled cards face down, one by one, 35 times and asking Pearce to write down what he thought each card was. The results showed that Pearce scored 22 million times better than could be expected by chance alone.

In 1925, Pagenstecher tested Spanish clairvoyant Maria Reyes by giving her in a sealed envelope a piece of paper he had been sent by a contact in the USA. Reyes reported seeing a large ship filled with people wearing lifejackets, all of whom were frightened. She said one man in particular stood out and that he was a tall man with black hair and moustache but a pale face. The paper was a note written to his wife by a man who was indeed tall and dark haired on board the liner *Lusitania* as it sank in 1915.

In 1977 scientists Russell Targ and Harold Puthoff of California's Stanford Research Institute announced that they had proved ESP to be true. They had carried out a series of tests in which those claiming ESP abilities were asked to identify a place at which Puthoff had gone to visit and was staring at. The pair produced results 500,000 times more accurate than chance alone. However, other scientists pointed out alleged flaws in the methodology of the tests that reduced the accuracy considerably.

DOWSING

In 1879 the Great Western Railway took over the East Somerset Railway and decided to enlarge the station at Shepton Mallet, which necessitated finding a source of water for the steam locomotives calling there. The engineers failed to find any local source of water and in desperation called in a local dowser named John Mullins. After two hours, Mullins pointed out a spot and a well was sunk that produced a regular flow of water. The fame of Mullins spread and thereafter he earned his living as a full-time dowser.

Dowsing depends on tiny involuntary movements of the shoulder muscles. These are magnified by the rod, pendulum or other object held by the dowser which then twitches, rotates or swings. What causes the shoulder muscles to move in the first place is unknown.

A group of German dowsers at work in the sixteenth century. German dowsers made a speciality of seeking veins of mineral rocks rather than water.

Frenchman Barthelemy Bleton of Dauphine claimed to be able to find any underground water. Brought to Paris he traced an underground water pipe across the gardens of the Luxembourg Palace while blindfolded.

In 1938 dowser L.L. Latham was hired to track the course of an old water culvert under Kensington Barracks. He tracked the culvert, but found it turned a number of odd corners as if avoiding some large, underground object. Excavations later showed the large object in question to be the concrete foundations of a Roman fortress.

POLITICIANS AND THE PARANORMAL

In April 1865 US President Abraham Lincoln had a remarkably vivid dream in which he had been walking around the White House when he heard the sound of weeping. Entering a room he saw a coffin draped in the US flag with a soldier mounting guard. The soldier turned to Lincoln and said, 'It is the president. He has been assassinated.' A few days later, Lincoln was shot dead.

William Lyon Mackenzie King served six terms as Canadian Prime Minister between 1921 and 1948. It was discovered only after his death that throughout this time King had been a firm believer in the paranormal. He frequently attended séances at which he sought to talk to deceased colleagues and often acted on hunches.

British Prime Minister Winston Churchill sometimes heard a disembodied voice giving him advice. In 1940 he interrupted a dinner party to hurry to the kitchen and evacuate staff. Moments later a bomb fell outside causing a blast that wrecked the kitchen, but not the dining room where Churchill and his guests were seated.

SPONTANEOUS HUMAN COMBUSTION

On 4 April 1731 Countess Cornelia de Bandi retired to bed at her home in Verona, Italy. Next morning the maid could smell burned clothing, entered the bedroom and found the countess's body beside her bed. 'There was a heap of ashes, two legs untouched with stockings on, between which lay the head, the brains, half of the back part of the skull and the whole chin burned to ashes, among which were found three fingers, blackened but intact.' A thin layer of soot was spread across the chamber. The jewels and other valuables were all untouched, ruling out the theory that she had been murdered by robbers and the body then burned.

On 22 March 1908 in Whitley Bay, Tyne and Wear, Margaret Dewar woke up smelling smoke. She tracked the smell to the bedroom of her sister, Wilhelmina. Margaret found her sister's body in its bed. The head and shoulders were intact, but the rest of the body had been turned to ash. The bedclothes adjacent to the body were also burned, but the bed had not caught fire. At the coroner's hearing, the coroner declared that the tale was impossible and refused to enter the circumstances in the official record. Instead he recorded a 'death by natural causes'.

On 1 July 1951, neighbours found the body of Mary Reeser at her home in St Petersburg, Florida. Mrs Reeser had been sitting in a chair when she died, and her body had been reduced utterly to ashes – though the chair was only lightly singed and no other object was burned. Dr Wilton Krogman, a forensic scientist who specialised in deaths by fire, was called. He estimated the heat needed to consume the body so completely to have been around 3,000° Fahrenheit, which would have burned the chair, carpet and so the entire house.

'Were I living in the Middle Ages, I would mutter something about black magic,' concluded Dr Krogman.

Dr John Irving Bentley of Coudersport, Pennsylvania, lived alone and could walk only with the aid of a Zimmer frame. On 5 December 1966, a gas company employee named Don Gosnell called to find Bentley's lower leg lying on the bathroom floor beside a pile of ash – which turned out to be the rest of Bentley's body. There was a hole in the floorboards, which had burned through, but otherwise there was no sign of a fire. A broken jug lay nearby as if Bentley had dropped it when he died.

On 13 September 1967 firemen were called to an empty house in London in which blue flames had been seen by a passer by. Entering the building they found the burning body of a tramp named Robert Bailey. Fireman Jack Stacey reported, 'There was a 4in slit in his abdomen from which was issuing, at force, a blue flame like a blowlamp. The flame was beginning to burn the wooden stairs. We extinguished the flames by placing a hose into the abdominal cavity. Bailey was alive when he started burning. He must have been in terrible pain. His teeth were sunk into the mahogany newel post of the staircase. I had to prise his jaws apart to release the body. The fire was coming from within the abdomen of his body.' The cause of death seemed to be smoke inhalation.

PSYCHOKINESIS

Psychokinesis (PK) is the alleged power to move objects using the power of thought alone. In the early 1970s American Felicia Parise reported that objects sometimes moved without her touching them, though she had no control over the phenomenon. Under controlled conditions she was asked to concentrate hard on small, light objects such as a plastic pill container and pieces of aluminum foil. She was able to move them, but soon pulled out of the tests saying that they left her utterly exhausted.

Indian holy man Swami Rama was studied at the Menninger Foundation in the 1970s. Swami Rama appeared to be able to move small objects, once causing a knitting needle to roll back and forth on a table. However, the tests were to study his ability to control his physiological functions and the psychokinetic feats were not pursued.

Russian housewife Ninel Kulagina was studied by Soviet scientists in the 1950s. She was shown to be able to move small objects a few inches on a table top, and movie film of her doing so still exists. She is also reported to have stopped the heart of a frog from beating. It is assumed that the Soviets spent so much time and money studying her gifts for sinister purposes – perhaps hoping to establish a team of PK assassins!

In the 1970s, English professor John Neihardt formed a group of twenty people to study the paranormal. At weekly meetings they tried to produce PK results. After many months the group claimed to be able to move a metal tray and make a doll hover in mid-air. The group then devised a 'PK Minilab' – a glass box that could be locked shut. Objects to be moved by PK were placed in the box so that they could not be touched.

In 1980 the idea of a PK Minilab was adopted by British researcher Julian Isaacs. He produced a series of evidence that seemed to indicate that PK was taking place.

PSYCHIC HEALING

Natasha Demkina who was born in 1987 in Saransk, a town 300 miles east of Moscow, has claimed to be able to see inside people's bodies. She has used this apparent gift to diagnose illnesses among the local people and so became known as 'the girl with x-ray eyes'. In 2004 she travelled to New York to be tested by a panel of doctors. Faced by seven individuals, she correctly diagnosed problems in four of them. The doctors considered this insufficient proof of any paranormal ability. Demkina returned to Russia where she began studies to become a doctor.

Rasputin the Russian monk is best known for his debauched lifestyle and the political power he gained in the final years of the Romanov dynasty in the early twentieth century. His power rested on the fact that he seemed able to alleviate and temporarily cure the haemophilia that affected the tsar's young son Alexei. Rasputin never revealed how he worked his cures, but some speculated it might be a form of hypnosis.

José Arigo of Brazil claimed to be able to cure the sick, but was put in prison after he was prosecuted for operating without a formal licence. Arigo claimed to have become aware of his gifts when visiting a sick relative. He became overwhelmed by the urge to cut the woman open, grabbed a knife and cut out a tumour, after which the woman recovered. Arigo said that when operating he was possessed by the spirit of a dead German physician, Dr Adolphus Fritz. After his eight months in prison in 1956, Arigo continued to practice, being imprisoned again in 1964. He died in a car crash in 1971.

8

GOING BEYOND

In the end, everyone dies. It is the only truly certain thing about life, and there is no escape. It is hardly surprising, therefore, that the subject of death and what happens to the person who dies has become a source of endless fascination to humans.

Most religions and philosophical systems have addressed the issue of what, if anything, happens to a human after death. Is death final, or is there some sort of survival? Nearly all religions hold that there is some immutable, eternal element inside a human being – Christians call it the soul – that survives the death of the physical body. Some religions teach that the soul goes on to another place, be it Heaven, the Elysian Fields, Valhalla or the Summerland. Other faiths believe that the soul returns to life, being reincarnated in another body on an endless cycle of life, death and rebirth.

Science has no real answer to the problem. Scientists can study the body, but are unable to account for the consciousness that sits within it. They can describe in detail how the body functions, but not what gives it the vital spark of life in the first place.

In recent years, however, there has been a growing body of evidence that has enabled some people to move beyond blind faith when it comes to what happens after death. Hints and clues that the soul does indeed move on have surfaced time and again. There is no firm proof, but the evidence is mounting.

MEDIUMS

A medium is a person who claims to be able to communicate with the dead. The conventional image of a medium is of a middle-aged lady swathed in floating robes sitting in darkness around a table together with those who wish to communicate with deceased loved ones. The medium then begins speaking, apparently passing on messages from the souls of the dead with whom she manages to get in contact.

While some mediums do match this image, many do not. While some prefer the tranquil setting of a quiet, dimly lit room in which to work, others find that a normally lit environment open to everyday noises and sounds is just as conducive to success. Some mediums work through spirit guides, a spirit with which they can make contact easily and who then passes on messages from the deceased; others speak directly to the spirits to be contacted. While many mediums use items or objects to help them concentrate, others do not. There are almost as many ways of working as there are mediums at work.

Karin Page founded the Star of the East spiritual healing centre in Kent after attending a spiritualist meeting. The medium, who Page had never met before told her that her mother-in-law had died recently from cancer and was named Mary, which was true. The medium claimed that Mary had a message of thanks to pass on, naming various members of Page's family. The message ended with Mary saying, 'I'm with Emma now.' At the time this meant nothing to Page, but she later learned that Emma had been Mary's sister but she had died many years earlier.

English medium Jill Nash has reported how one day she received a visit from an elderly lady, but that the lady arrived with a male companion. The sitting opened with the man saying he wanted to tell the lady about a feature of their garden – at which point it became clear that the man was the lady's deceased husband and that she had no idea that he was there.

In October 1930, renowned psychic investigator Harry Price arranged for medium Eileen Garrett to hold a séance with a number of witnesses. During the séance Garrett apparently made contact with an RAF officer named Flight Lieutenant H. Carmichael Irwin, who said he had been on board the *R101* airship which had crashed in mysterious circumstances a few days earlier. Price passed the notes on to one of the engineers who had built the airship. The information passed on by Garrett proved to be both highly technical and absolutely accurate. The spirit of Irwin had gone on to describe the final minutes before the crash and to identify the cause of the disaster. Although these claims could not be verified, they did match the evidence of the wreckage.

Helen Duncan was a medium who made headlines in 1944 by being the last woman ever to be charged under the Witchcraft Act of 1735 in the UK. Found guilty of 'falsely claiming superhuman powers that do not come from God', she was imprisoned for nine months. The trial followed séances at which Duncan had claimed to make contact with sailors killed during the fighting in the Second World War. Duncan had announced the names of ships sunk or damaged and where they were before the news was released by the government. It is generally thought that the government was worried that the news announced by Duncan might be of use to the enemy, and so had arranged the prosecution to keep her quiet.

Madame Helena Petrovna Blavatsky was hugely controversial in her lifetime, and has remained so to this day. She was born in Russia in 1831, claimed to have travelled extensively through Asia and North Africa in search of spiritual powers and went on to found the Theosophical Movement in an attempt to blend Christianity and eastern religions. In 1885 the Society for Psychical Research (SPR) produced a report by Richard Hodgson that denounced Blavatsky as a fraud. She was said to have plagiarised nearly all of her writings, to have faked events at séances and to have lied extensively about her background.

However, in 1986 the SPR retracted the Hodgson report, after a re-examination of the case by the psychic Dr Vernon Harrison.

'Madame Blavatsky,' the new statement read, 'was unjustly condemned.'

The nineteenth-century Scottish medium Daniel Douglas Home was famous for the wide range of his mediumistic abilities. Not content with merely communicating with the deceased, he would enliven his séances with spectral lights and music while apparently shrinking or enlarging his body and limbs.

OUIJA BOARDS

The ouija takes its name from the fact that early versions had the words written in both French and German so the box for 'yes' read 'oui ja'. The users place a glass or pointer on the board, which is marked with letters and with commonly used words. The board is supposed to help channel messages from the spirit world. The glass or pointer will move around the board apparently of its own volition to spell out words and phrases. It was popularised as a game in the 1890s by the Fuld company of Maryland and is still sometimes sold as a game despite the growing sinister reputation that it has acquired.

In 1913 Mrs Pearl Curran used a ouija board to contact a spirit that claimed to be Patience Worth who had lived in Dorset and North America in the seventeenth century. Using the ouija, Curran produced a vast amount of poetry apparently composed by Worth. More than 1.6 million words of poetry and historical fiction were eventually produced, and published under the name of Worth.

In 1917 Emily Hutchings claimed to have contacted American writer Mark Twain, who had recently died, through a ouija

board. Using the board, Hutchings produced a novel that she claimed had been written by Twain. When she tried to publish the book as by Mark Twain, the Twain family took her to court arguing that the book was so awful that it could not possibly have been written by Twain. The court agreed.

REINCARNATION

Hinduism, Buddhism and some other religions teach that the human soul does not cease to exist at death, but instead passes into another body so that it can live again. The teachings are not identical, but do share the feature that the person's essential being is thought to continue to exist beyond death and to be recycled.

The current Dalai Lama, Tenzin Gyatso, is believed by followers to be the thirteenth reincarnation of the first Dalai Lama, Gendun Drup, who died in 1474. The position of Dalai Lama is the supreme chief of Buddhism in Tibet and formerly combined this role with that of head of the government. Whenever a Dalai Lama died, the chief priests would seek out his reincarnation in a boy born soon after the Dalai Lama's death. After consulting visions, dreams and portents, the boy would be presented with personal possessions of the former Dalai Lama to see how he responded.

The American Second World War general George Patton was a firm believer in reincarnation. More than once he expressed the opinion that he was the reincarnation of the ancient Carthaginian general Hannibal. Since Hannibal is widely believed to have been one of the greatest military men who ever lived, this claim was treated as boasting by several colleagues.

Motor car magnate Henry Ford was born in 1863 just four weeks after the Battle of Gettysburg, the bloodiest and most decisive battle in the American Civil War. At the age of twenty-eight he became convinced that he was the reincarnation of a soldier killed at Gettysburg, and held this belief until he died in 1947.

PAST LIVES REGRESSION

Under hypnosis people are often able to remember events in great detail that they cannot recall at all in their normal state. This process is known as regression hypnosis and can be useful for various therapies and treatments. However, one practitioner, Arnall Bloxham, experimented with regressing patients back beyond their birth. The startling result was that many patients began talking about previous lives that they claimed to have lived before their current life. Since Bloxham publicised his findings in the book *The Bloxham Tapes* in 1976, other hypnotists have achieved similar results.

Under hypnosis Ann Evans remembered a previous life as Rebecca, a young Jewish woman living in Yorkshire in the twelfth century. This life ended violently when Rebecca was killed during anti-Jewish riots that occurred in York in 1189. According to Evans, Rebecca was killed when rioters broke into her hiding place, the crypt of St Mary's Church in the city – but this church had no crypt so the story seemed to be disproved. However, some years after Rebecca told her tale a long-forgotten crypt was discovered under St Mary's.

When hypnotised, Californian housewife Barbara Larson remembered the long life of Sam Sneed, a man who started his career as a gambler on the river boats in the 1870s, moved on to be a salesman and ended as a respected citizen of Sacramento. The memories were vivid and consistent, but there is no evidence that a man named Sam Sneed ever existed.

In 1969 Joanne McIver regressed to remember the life of Susan Ganier who lived in rural Ontario from 1835 to 1903. She recalled her childhood, marriage, the death of her husband and a long, uneventful widowhood. A search of Ontario's archives soon revealed that Susan Ganier had lived as had several of the other people mentioned by McIver. When she visited Ontario, McIver recognised several old buildings and correctly named buildings long since demolished but known from old maps.

CHILDHOOD MEMORIES OF ADULT LIFE

Some children claim to be able to remember a previous life when they were adults. Typical was the case of a four-year-old child living in Delhi by the name of Shanti Deva. In 1930, Shanti suddenly announced that she could remember living in a place called Muttra and that she had three children there. She also said that her name was Ludgi and she had died in agony during childbirth. Shanti's father investigated and found that there was a village called Muttra where a woman named Ludgi had died a few weeks before Shanti was born. He arranged for a man living in Muttra to send him a list of twenty-four questions to which only Ludgi or a member of her close family would know the answer. Shanti got them all correct. As she grew older, Shanti's memories of a previous life faded away.

In Lebanon, Imad Elawar began remembering a previous life at the age of three. By the age of five the boy could recall a great amount of detail about his former life. When questioned by researcher Dr Ian Stevenson in 1976, Imad gave fifty-seven pieces of information about his previous life. Stevenson then drove to the village named by Imad as his former home and found two people named by Imad. Between them they confirmed about two-thirds of the claims made by the boy and were unable to contradict any of the others.

In 1957 tragedy struck the Pollock family of Hexham, Northumberland, when a car crash claimed the lives of the two daughters Joanna, eleven, and Jacqueline, six. The family moved away and the following year Mrs Pollock gave birth to twin girls. One girl, Jennifer, had an identical birthmark to the deceased Jacqueline. In 1962 the Pollocks paid a visit to Hexham, and the girls were able to point out their parents' old home and the school that had been attended by Joanna and Jacqueline. The girls also developed a fear of cars. When shown old toys of their deceased elder sisters, the girls correctly identified the dolls by name. After the age of five the apparent memories faded and then vanished.

NEAR-DEATH EXPERIENCE

Some people claim after recovering from a serious illness or life-threatening injury that they experienced a sensation that they had died and their souls had moved on from their bodies. Such experiences might be dismissed as being hallucinations brought on by shock or trauma were it not for the fact that they are so often consistent. Different people, who usually have no knowledge of the experiences of others, report the same events time after time.

Of particular interest to researchers is the fact that the experiences do not correlate with the person's religion. If a Christian reported having met Christ or St Peter, for instance, and a Hindu reported meeting Vishnu then these accounts might be written off as having been prompted by the person's individual beliefs, but again this is not the case. The experiences that are reported seem to be entirely independent of the percipient's religious beliefs, if any.

Doctors and others had been sporadically recording NDEs among survivors for many years, but it was not until 1975 when Raymond Moody Jr published a book on the subject entitled *Life after Life*, that the subject was taken seriously.

The International Association for Near-Death Studies (IANDS) was set up in the USA in 1981 and has since grown to have associated bodies in more than two dozen other countries. It maintains an archive of NDE accounts and provides advice and support to those who have experienced an NDE.

These events are termed Near-Death Experiences, or NDE. A typical NDE goes through a number of steps or stages:

1   The typical NDE begins with the percipient realising that they are dead. This is often, but not always, accompanied by a deeply unpleasant noise or shaking sensation.

2   The second stage begins with a feeling of calm as worries and unpleasant feelings seem to drift away.

3   Thirdly the percipients feel as if they are floating out of their bodies. Sometimes this is a generalised feeling of weightlessness, but a few people report actually seeing their body and its surroundings as if they are floating a few feet up in the air.

4   Fourthly the person feels that they are being drawn irresistibly towards a dark doorway or opening that leads into a long tunnel or passageway. At the far end of the tunnel there is a bright light. Some people feel that they are being drawn upwards through this tunnel, others that they are sliding down it.

5   Towards the far end of the dark tunnel, most people report meeting a person. This person may be a friend or relative who is already dead or a complete stranger. A small number of percipients report meeting a person that they feel is holy or divine, but without identifying them in an particular way. There usually – but not always – follows a conversation at this point. The percipient is told that everything is going to be alright and that they should not worry, although a few have reported that they are threatened and verbally abused.

6   Once the conversation is over, the NDE proceeds to the sixth commonly reported stage. The percipient drifts out of the tunnel and into a wide, open area that is brightly lit and usually white or pale yellow. Here the person may experience flashbacks to various episodes in their lives, reliving events that generally have some strong emotional meaning for them.

7   After all this, the percipient comes to a second doorway, which is usually locked shut and cannot be opened.

Only a small minority of percipients report reaching as far as the second door and, so far as is known, none have reported going further. At some point along the journey, the percipient starts to feel uncomfortable, as if they are in the wrong place. Some feel that they should return back to their bodies, others report being told to do so by a person that they meet. This is followed by a dizzying sensation akin to being whirled around or by the feeling of sudden and very rapid movement. The percipients then wake up back in their bodies.

A study of heart patients who had suffered severe heart attacks and been revived was carried out in 2001 by Dutch cardiac surgeon Pim van Lommel. He found that 18 per cent of those who had nearly died had experienced a Near-Death Experience that closely matched the typical progression. The others recalled nothing.

The *Journal of Near-Death Studies* is published quarterly by Allen Press. It includes academic, peer-reviewed papers and studies on the subject of Near-Death Experiences.

In 2005 an Australian research team conducted a telephone survey and found that 8.9 per cent of the population had experienced an NDE at some point in their lives.

OCT   2013